DISCERNMENT

ACQUIRING THE HEART OF GOD

Marko Ivan Rupnik

auline
BOOKS & MEDIA
Boston

Library of Congress Cataloging-in-Publication Data
Rupnik, Marko Ivan, 1954–
  [Discernimento. English]
  Discernment : acquiring the heart of God / Marko Ivan Rupnik. — 1st English ed.
     p. cm.
  Includes bibliographical references.
  ISBN 0-8198-1882-8 (pbk.)
  1. Discernment of spirits. 2. Christian life—Catholic authors. I. Title.
  BV5083.R8713 2006
  248.4'82—dc22

                                                    2005028069

The Scripture quotations contained herein are from the *New Revised Standard Version Bible: Catholic Edition,* copyright © 1989, 1993, Division of Christian Education of the National Council of the Churches of Christ in the United States of America. Used by permission. All rights reserved.

Cover design by Rosana Usselmann

Cover art by Mystic Artist Rassouli (www.Rassouli.com)

Translated by Susan Dawson Vásquez

Originally published in Italian under the titles *Il discernimento: Verso il gusto di Dio* (volume 1) and *Il discernimento: Come rimanere con Cristo* (volume 2) by Lipa srl, 25 Paolina, Roma. All rights reserved.

First English edition, 2006

Published by Pauline Books & Media, 50 Saint Paul's Avenue, Boston, MA 02130-3491.

Printed in the U.S.A.

www.pauline.org

Pauline Books & Media is the publishing house of the Daughters of St. Paul, an international congregation of women religious serving the Church with the communications media.

2 3 4 5 6 7 8 9   20 19 18 17 16

Contents

Part II

HOW TO REMAIN WITH CHRIST

Introduction

A soul is perfect whose sensitive powers tend wholly toward God.
— Maximus the Confessor[1]

FOR QUITE A FEW YEARS NOW, people have begun speaking once again about discernment. Discernment is the art of knowing Christ and recognizing him as our Lord and Savior. The Church, through her tradition and the teaching of her pastors, has developed and preserved this understanding of discernment in the Church as it has developed through the centuries. However, although this primary sense of discernment is important for the Church's interest, for ecclesial communities, and for people's individual lives with all their concrete significance, discernment can actually be spoken of in a variety of ways. For example, there is also the discernment of spirits. "To another [is given] discernment of spirits," says the Apostle (cf. 1 Cor 12:10). Then there is the discernment of our inner movements, of our thoughts and feelings, and there is the discernment of vocations, of states of life, etc. There is the discernment made by individuals and by communities. There is also a discernment that is more strictly concerned with morals.[2]

This book explores discernment, drawing out its dynamics as the art of communication between God and

1

us, as the art of reciprocal understanding. This approach considers in an interrelated way the various forms of discernment mentioned.

If we seek to study discernment as the communication between God and persons, we will need to study it in two stages, since each stage has a different dynamic. The first stage is the stage of purification, which leads one to an authentic knowledge of self-in-God and of God in one's personal history. This stage is covered in Part I of this volume. In the second stage, discernment becomes a habit. This stage is taken up in Part II.

Discernment is not a technique for resolving the problems of one's spiritual life, but a reality found in the relationship between the human person and God.

Part I unfolds the first stage of discernment in three chapters. Chapter 1 offers the theological references that constitute the framework for discernment, that is, that understanding of God and the person upon which is built reciprocal communication and understanding in love and freedom. Chapter 2 explains discernment. Finally, Chapter 3 introduces the dynamics of the first phase of discernment.

Part II treats remaining united to Christ, how to hold on to what has been attained through the work of Part I. Here we will deal with discernment as the art of following Christ, both in the larger choices in life and work, and in smaller daily decisions. We will find that the further we progress in the spiritual life, the more temptations are camouflaged. That is why discernment in the following of Christ consists in great part in unmasking illusions and in orienting ourselves to the realism and objectivity of Christ our Lord and Savior, the paschal Messiah who lives in the Church and in history. Discernment, in fact, leads to an ecclesial maturity, to a proven faithfulness.

For this reason, Part II opens with Chapter 4, which is dedicated to the theological principle and foundation of remaining in Christ. Chapters 5 and 6 will take up the temptations that Christians experience in following the Lord, describing the tempter's delusions and principal mechanisms and laying out the manner in which the spiritual Fathers unmasked these deceptions. Chapter 7 is dedicated to showing how to verify one's true surrender to Christ, so that there is no space for illusions or deceptions. Since discernment is not a technique for resolving the problems of one's spiritual life, but a reality found in the relationship between the human person and God—in the space, therefore, of love—it is necessary to be initiated into the first steps in the exercise of discernment. What is explained in Chapter 8 are the most suitable circumstances and most appropriate ways to begin the art of discernment, concluding with Chapters 9 and 10, which deal with two of the most meaningful elements of the second stage, that is, the discernment of a vocation and communal discernment. From the entire journey, it becomes evident that true discernment is a constant attitude.

Throughout the entire text, almost parallel with each subheading, references will be given—mainly from Ignatius of Loyola and the philokalic authors. These spiritual masters constitute, together with study and years of pastoral practice, the ambiance in which these reflections have developed.[3]

It is important to state that, no matter how useful *reading* about discernment can be, discernment is a reality into which one must be initiated. This initiation requires a rational-experiential approach. Reading this book, therefore, cannot dispense the reader from learning discernment at the side of a mentor, walking along a sometimes difficult path that progressively conforms one to the Lord.

PART I
Acquiring God's Tastes

CHAPTER 1

The Basis of Discernment

IS IT POSSIBLE FOR A REAL RELATIONSHIP between God and the human person to exist? If so, in what does it consist? Can God and someone truly communicate with and understand one another? What language do they use when they communicate? Is the language univocal, analogical, or dialectical? Does God command while people simply obey and carry out orders? Or, rather, do people on their own decide what might please God based on what they know of the divine commandments and then carry that out? Within the great divine design, is there a space for human autonomy?

The masters of the spiritual life would not approve of beginning our study of discernment by asking these questions that speak of God and the person as two separate realities. Through the work of the Holy Spirit we share in the Father's love through his Son, Jesus Christ.[1] This grace—that is, the presence of God's love in us—makes possible our access to God and to other people created in this love. And that is not all. Such divine indwelling in us means that God is no longer outside our human reality, but becomes—as Pavel Evdokimov says—an internal fact of our nature.[2]

Therefore, true communication exists between the Lord and us. To assure the freedom of this communication, we must make use of human thoughts and feelings. The Fathers, who usually opted for symbolic language as the language that best expressed divine-human communication,[3] described discernment as prayer, truly an art of living *in* the Holy Spirit. So at this point we can define discernment as part of a lived relationship between God and the human person in which one experiences this relationship with God as one of freedom, a relationship in which one even has the possibility of creating oneself. In this sense, discernment is the art in which humans disclose themselves in the creativity of history and create history by creating themselves.

> In discernment, one enters into a free relationship not only with God, but also with others and even with creation... [that is] a living relationship with all that exists.

Discernment, therefore, is a relational reality, just as is faith itself. The Christian faith is a relational reality, because the God who reveals himself to us communicates himself with love, and love presupposes the recognition of a "Thou."[4] God is Love because God is absolute communication, eternal relationship, both in the primordial act of the reciprocal love of the three divine Persons as well as in creation. In discernment, therefore, one enters into a free relationship not only with God, but also with others and even with creation, for from the moment one enters into an authentic relationship with God, one enters into an optic of love that is a living relationship with all that exists.

Having this vision means understanding the interweaving of threads that bind together and connect every part of creation, and from which emerge the essential communion of everything that exists. From the moment that we see the divine reality, all these "threads"—their presence in things, in objects, and in the products of human making—instill in everything new meaning, because all things and all actions are capable of assuming a more profound significance. This is an essentially *sacramental* vision of the world by which, through the things we see, we have access to their truth.[5] We can now say that discernment is thus the art of understanding oneself while keeping this overall cohesive structure in mind, of seeing oneself in unity because one sees with God's eyes, eyes that see the unity of life.

Understanding Ourselves in Relationship with God

We believe in God the Father, the Son, and the Holy Spirit. God as an ideal or a concept would not be of great significance for us Christians. We Christians are such because Revelation communicates to us a God who is Three in One. Invoking each Person, we are, in fact, calling on the one God, since each Person exists in a relationship of indissoluble and complete unity with the other two. When we affirm belief in God the Father, we are saying at the same time that we believe in the Holy Spirit and in the Son. The same holds for each of the divine Persons: the reference to each of them automatically embraces their trinitarian communion, referring back to the other two.

In this sense, the first article of the Creed is of primary importance: "I believe in one God, *the Father.*"

To affirm belief simply in God is much more ambiguous than to affirm belief in God the Father. It would be an affirmation about God open to different interpretations, understandings, and even idolatries—from ideas to concepts to figures to rites, from abstraction on one end to a reality that is strictly sensory on the other. Believing in God the Father, however, further signifies that God is truly a reality, that he is beyond any possible manipulation, because "Father" signifies a person, and a person is not a concept but an actual reality.[6]

Saying "Father" indicates a Face, and a face—even if never seen—is always actual and conveys a precise personal reality that is objective in itself. In saying "Father," we acknowledge the reality of God in three Persons, as well as the reality of their relationship. At the same time, however, to say "I believe in God the Father," also means affirming an actual identity, revealing an actual Face, because those who pronounce the word "Father" declare themselves children, a relationship revealed precisely by virtue of God's revelation as Father.[7]

The article of faith "I believe in one God the Father" points out the relationship that exists between us and God, which is precisely a child-parent relationship. Faith, therefore, is our relationship to God as children. This means then that we cannot approach the question of faith with principles or an abstract terminology.

Love Made Real Through Gratuitous Relationships

This God in whom we believe is a Person. We contemplate and adore this God as the Three in One. The three Persons in God give themselves to each other entirely and with complete freedom. In God exists the most perfect communication. The Three in One reveals himself above all as the absence of necessity. In God, each Person gives himself to the others in an absolutely gratuitous love beyond every law of necessity. When John says that God is love, he affirms that God is free and that love entails adhering freely to the other in love, relating to the other with freedom. Without a relationship of freedom, it is impossible to love. It would be something else all together.

In God the three Persons not only love each other, but each Person also loves the divine nature each of them possesses whole and entire.[8] Thus each divine Person possesses the nature of God, giving him an entirely personal mark—of the Father, or of the Son, or of the Holy Spirit—in such a way that their relationship also includes the nature that all the Persons possess completely, each in his own way. It is a complex relationship, but a completely gratuitous one, an attachment so gratuitous that John can say, God *is* love.

God's relationship in his most holy Persons is a communication not only in the sense that the divine Persons communicate *between* themselves, but also, above all, in the sense that they *communicate themselves* in a reciprocal love, giving themselves to each other in love. This intradivine communication is not separate from God's communication toward his creation. God not only communicates *with* creation—and above all with humans as created persons—but he *communicates himself*. It is only because God is love that we can come to know God, because love means relationship, that is, *communication*, that is, to *communicate one's self*.[9]

Our knowledge of God is not, therefore, a theoretical, abstract knowledge, but a communicative knowledge, a knowledge within which a self-communication takes place. God communicates himself in a personal way in the gratuitous relationship he has with us. The Holy Spirit—the communicator par excellence of the Most Holy Trinity to the created world—makes God known to us in a personal way, that is, by communicating his life to us in grace. To know God's presence we need to adopt an attitude of awareness.

Such awareness, which we can call sapiential-symbolic, leads to a *life* similar to God's life. Awareness of God is thus also a communication of the art of living. God communicates his likeness to the human person on a created level. The person is made in the image of God. But through the redemption brought about by God himself, and through the Holy Spirit, who communicates to us the salvation won for us by Christ, we are able to know God and to become aware of this knowledge as itself a likeness to God.

God, in a certain sense, communicates to humanity God's own way of being, which is love. Therefore, the human person becomes like God when his or her life is lived in the way of love, that is, in communion, in the image of the Trinity. This way of communion is the life of the Church, of the community; thus it is true that it is the Church that gives birth to us as believers.

To Believe Is to Love

The awareness of God is not, therefore, an abstract theoretical knowledge to which can be given a practical, ethical-moral interpretation. God, the Three in One, can never be reduced to a doctrine, to a list of precepts, or to an ascetic effort, but is known only within a reciprocal self-communication where the absolute initiative belongs to the relationship of love gratuitously offered by God the Father to which one responds with an act of faith that is actually, as we have seen, a relational act. It is an act that is, at the same time, one of love and of freedom, since it knows the Other, God, in all his absolute Otherness and surrenders to God to the point of radically orienting oneself to God.[10] Faith as a radical affirmation of the Other, of God, means adhering with all of one's self to God's absolute Otherness. Even faith as content, as teaching, as men-tality, and as moral life discloses itself to humanity only through love, that is, through an attitude of recognition, ecstasy, reaching out, and orienting self toward the Other. This is because in God—with a properly theological understanding of Person—*everything* is comprehensible only through love and surrender.

Thus it can be said that the objectivity of the Other—of God or of another person—means precisely that I can never possess them. It is impossible to say that one truly believes in God without love, which is the only force after sin that is capable of shifting us away from ourselves and radically orienting us to the other.[11] Believing in God the Father, Son, and Holy Spirit means *loving* God the Father, Son, and Holy Spirit. This already involves a style of life. In fact, believing in God, knowing God, and loving God are realities that can be understood and realized only within an actual lived experience that moves within a tradition, within the Church.

The division that exists between believing and loving is the gravely harmful effect of sin, which produces within us a multitude of other divisions, other fractures. We often throw ourselves into eradicating this inner diversion through dogmatism, moralism, psychologism, and various other "isms"—only to discover that we have been deluded. Believing in God, knowing God—precisely because it is possible to do so only by loving God and opening oneself to the Spirit—entails a conversion. It is a renunciation of the principle of evil—the principle of death constituted by sin—by radically and freely choosing God as the supreme good because he is tri-personal love.[12]

> Belief is only possible if we allow ourselves to be penetrated by God's love, precisely because faith grows from love.

Belief is only possible, therefore, if we allow ourselves to be penetrated by God's love, precisely because faith grows from love.[13] In First Corinthians 13, Paul does not say "if I have not loved," but "if I have not love," which means that God creates us by giving us his own love and that a person exists only insofar as the Holy Spirit makes God's love dwell in him or her. Love is not the person's initiative but a welcoming of God's gift.

Sin has isolated us from God's love. People attempt to live their lives outside love, giving in to that dimension that Paul calls the "flesh." For Paul, "flesh" is the vulnerable part of us that perceives our fragility and death and wants to save us by having us affirm ourselves in an exclusive, unilateral manner, seeking ourselves in created things and in our relationships with others. The flesh, in fact, means rebellion against the spirit, that is, against that dimension of the human person that is capable of opening the self to God's Spirit, who by his action dwells in the person. The flesh is rebellion against openness, against real relationship, against agape, against charity. It is the renunciation of the "intelligence" of love.

There is a great risk that we will even seek to understand God in this *self*-affirming way, that we will wind up imprisoning God himself. We can extract ourselves from this unredeemed reality only with difficulty. In this delusion of self-affirmation, we become the ones who give form and content to God's revelation. It is even possible to think of God from the viewpoint of the flesh, that is, with that intelligence which reasons according to the criteria of the flesh. There is perhaps nothing worse than thinking of God with an intelligence exercised in a reductive way, with a fractured rationality. Signs of this reductionism are attitudes of domination, of possession, of attempting to exhaust all possibilities with regard to God, and feelings of omnipotence.

The main trap into which we can fall and by which we can allow ourselves to be deceived is that of developing a perfect, impeccable "logic" that protects us from surprises, encloses us within the "castle" of our own opinions and prejudices, and makes us out to be all-knowing and omnipotent. Because of its inherent dualism, after having fallen into this trap, we find ourselves in a quandary when we are unable to settle the question of freedom. This dualism seeks to arrange freedom for itself, but it actually does not promote complete surrender. Because it doesn't inflame the heart within an integrally human desire, this dualism doesn't bring about authentic conversion, but seeks personal improvement by ethical principles and moral imperatives. In the end, the person in this trap becomes exhausted by failure and sinks more and more into compromises, because the person discovers it is impossible to live according to the proposed ideal or to lower his or her ideal in order not to suffer from ethical failure.

In other words, false freedom triggers the thought that *we* can reach the knowledge of God, decipher God's will, deduce moral and ascetic steps to improve ourselves *without the experience of being redeemed,* that is, without the experience of the reawakening that only the love of God dwelling in us is capable of bringing about. Only the love of God can make us feel complete and turn us toward gratuitous relationships, both with God as well as with others. If our knowledge of God is not derived from the experience of his love for us, felt and understood in the act of redemption, it is an illusion or the swelling of the selfish idolatry of our own reason.

Here we should certainly recall Jeremiah 31:34, where the prophet proclaims that the fruit of the new alliance formed with the house of Israel will be a knowledge of the Lord based on the experience of his mercy: "No longer shall they teach one another, or say to each other, 'Know the LORD,' for they shall all know me, from the least of them to the greatest, says the LORD; for I will forgive their iniquity, and remember their sin no more." This is the same reality announced in First John 4, which clearly explains that it is impossible to love God except on the basis of being loved by him.

Discernment as the Acceptance of My Salvation

Discernment is thus the art of the spiritual life in which I understand how God communicates himself to me, how God saves me—and this is the same thing—how God brings about redemption through the life, death, and resurrection of his Son, and how the Holy Spirit communicates to me the salvation won for me by Jesus Christ. Discernment is the art in which I freely give myself to a God who, in Jesus, freely entrusted himself into my hands. It is an art, therefore, in which the realities in creation, the realities in the persons around me, the realities within me, and the realities in my personal history and in history itself cease being mute in order to begin to communicate to me God's love.[14] And this is not all. Discernment is also that spiritual art by which I am able to avoid deception and illusions, to decipher and "read" reality in a true way, seeing through and rejecting what are revealed as empty promises. Discernment is the art of speaking directly with God, not with temptations or with those temptations about God.

Avoiding Illusions about Love

Discernment is the expression of a contemplative intelligence. It is an art that presupposes knowing how to contemplate, knowing how to see God. Now, God is love, and we know that love is fulfilled in the way of Christ and the Holy Spirit, who both reveal the Father to us. Therefore, love always has a *paschal* dimension and a *pentecostal* dimension. The paschal dimension is sacrifice and offering—as the relationship between the

Father and the Son represents the tragic side of love—
and a dimension of overcoming death and tragedy, of
the fulfillment of sacrificial love. Love is fulfilled in the
resurrection, in everlasting life, in celebration, because
love is answered, and thus it is possible to live the fullness of surrender, the pentecostal dimension represented by the Holy Spirit, the Comforter, Love of love,
the hypostatic joy of the Father for the Son and of the
Son for the Father.[15] It is
neither easy to understand
nor to accept the love that is
fulfilled in a paschal and
pentecostal way, that is, in
the way of sacrifice and
resurrection. In fact, even
historically the work of
God's love realized in Christ
was understood and accepted after Pentecost only
thanks to the Holy Spirit. It
is precisely an intelligence
that penetrates these realities that we call "contemplative," that is, an intelligence that works in synergy with
the Holy Spirit.

> For the most part, peo-
> ple do everything they
> can to avoid the pas-
> chal path, but every
> such attempt...empties
> existence of the true
> flavor of life.

Human intelligence is used in the most complete and
total manner only when all its cognitive capacities
converge in an intellect that is illuminated, opened, and
guided by the Holy Spirit. The contemplative person is
the one who can see with the luminous eye of the Holy
Spirit. Only in this way can a person see that God's will
coincides with God's love and that such love is fulfilled
in the death and resurrection of Christ.

For the most part, people do everything they can to avoid the paschal path, but every such attempt sooner or later shows itself to be an illusion that hardens the heart and empties existence of the true flavor of life. That is why it helps to choose the path of discernment, which is the contemplative and wise path. Everything beautiful, good, noble, and just is played out in the midst of difficulties, obstacles, and resistance and thus assumes a paschal dimension. The path of the Holy Spirit never passes from Holy Thursday to Easter Sunday, skipping over Good Friday and Holy Saturday. In order to understand this, however, it takes true contemplation and great capacity for discernment.

At times, to avoid the path of true faith—the path of love for God, the path of true conversion—we propose high ideals, projects that go beyond even what the Gospel proposes, more than the imitation of the greatest saints. Then afterward, bitter, tired, and deluded, we reject not only the proposed ideals we have made but also our faith, or we become closed, hardened, and harsh with everyone who doesn't do as we do. Discernment protects us from deviations ranging from fundamentalism to fanaticism precisely because it teaches us that what *we* decide to do is never as important as doing things in a free surrender to God, in harmony with his will. Since God's will is love, it is difficult to carry it out while asserting our own wills, even if our wills are marked with sacrosanct labels.

Many people, for example, have decided to live radical poverty, perhaps a poverty even greater than that of St. Francis, but nothing has come of it. Radicalism is not important in itself, but only as a response to God's love. Spiritually meaningful things never happened in the Church because someone decided to do them, but because God found someone available to welcome him in such a radical way that he could manifest himself and carry out *his* redemption.

Discovering Our Vocation

The human person was created through the sharing of the love of God the Father.[16] The Holy Spirit made this love dwell in the person, imprinting the image of the Son. In fact, the Fathers of the Church say that we were created "in the Son."[17] The creation of humanity is thus the work of the love of the Three in One.[18] Redemption itself is an act of the same love. It enables us to share in the full realization of God's love in the form of Christ, to the point of the fullness of our relationship as children of God, which is realized in communion with our brothers and sisters, among persons who live relationships as brothers and sisters because they are sons and daughters who, in Christ, turn to the Father. It is against this background of creation and redemption that vocation is understood.[19]

Humanity exists because God has spoken the word, has called us into existence, making us his interlocutors. Our vocation is the word that God speaks to humanity and that makes us exist, imprinting on us his dialogical mark. It can almost be said, along with Nikolai Berdiaev,[20] that the vocation precedes the person. Our lives can be understood as the time we are given for this dialogue with God. If we are created through this conversation with God and are thus called to speak, to express and communicate ourselves, and to respond, then the time we have at our disposal can be understood as the time for realizing this vocation.

Now, in what does the human vocation consist? Again, in First Corinthians 13 Paul very clearly points out that what we do without love is worth nothing. It is wasted, lost. We could even make heroic, unheard-of sacrifices, have faith strong enough to move mountains, but if we do not have love, these are worthless. The human vocation, thus, is truly a life in love, a life in that love in which we were created and that was made possible anew through the redemption. Our vocation therefore is the full realization of humanity in love, within the dialogical principle in which we were created, with God as the prime Interlocutor.

> Discernment helps me to sanctify the time God has given to me to fulfill myself in Christ.

Discernment can thus be defined as that art through which a person understands the word addressed to him or her, a word in which is revealed the path that must be traveled to respond to the Word.[21] Discernment helps me to sanctify the time God has given to me to fulfill my vocation, which is love, and, therefore, to fulfill myself in Christ who is the full realization of love in his paschal sacrifice. My vocation is not an automatic fact but a process of maturing in relationships, beginning with the foundational relationship with God. It is a progressive seeing myself and my history with God's eyes. It is seeing how God realizes himself in me and in others, and how I can open myself to this work in such a way that I become part of the humanity assumed by Christ and through which creation is also assumed in order to offer everything to the Father.

In the Church, on the Trail of Tradition

In the dialogue with God, in the conversation with our Creator and Redeemer, none of us is alone. We are already preceded by a long memory of the wisdom of how to open ourselves to love so as not to fall into the trap of wanting to serve love by self-affirmation. Wisdom is the tradition of the Church, a living fabric, an organism that makes the revelation of God's word come alive not only as Scripture, but also as its many interpretations and inculturations in the lives of the generations of Christians who have preceded us. This is the memory of holiness we draw upon through spiritual initiation.[22]

The spiritual life is learned in a sapiential way, that is, from persons. In this way the risk of remaining in ideologies and theorizing is avoided, and there emerges a logic born of life and a life illuminated by an intellect guided by the Holy Spirit.[23] Images, forms, flavors, and tastes are all important for the memory, all actual realities, just as God's Face is, and are found in the communion of the saints. On the other hand, the Christian does not exist if not in the Church; since if to believe means to love, the true realization of faith is the community, and its true expression is the art of spiritual relationships. The Christian inserted within a community participates in the life of the Church and listens to her pastors, the primary fathers in the faith. In listening to them and in union with them, participating in the life of charity, the life of the Christian flows into the liturgy, where the love of God the Father is truly communicated through redemption in Christ and the action of the Holy Spirit, which makes all these holy realities present and personal. It is within this environment that one can come to know whether a discernment is true or false, since every true discernment brings one the celebration of Christ in the Church.

In her tradition, liturgy, and magisterium, the Church brings to fulfillment and expresses her discernment about Christ and the salvation that continues to flow from God's heart for all people of all times. Personal discernment allows this to become—for real people in real situations—a truly lived experience. People welcome their salvation responsibly and freely and adhere to Christ, their Savior and Lord, with their choices and attitudes, with concrete steps that permeate their entire beings, even their ways of thinking and their cultures. They weave their stories into the fabric of the Church, not as the sum of individuals with their individual stories, but as a living, communitarian organism, precisely because each one has accepted salvation.

CHAPTER 2

What Is Discernment?

How We Know Ourselves

BETWEEN GOD AND EVERY PERSON there is a real relationship and consequently true communication. How does God speak to us? Through our very thoughts and feelings. God does not act in us as something foreign, introducing realities that are not our own. Because God is love, and because we participate in this love in the Holy Spirit, it is the Spirit who acts as our most intimate reality. The Holy Spirit works in us through love as our most authentic identity. We perceive the Holy Spirit's action as our own truth precisely because it is an action of love.

Thoughts inspired by the Spirit, therefore, or the feelings God inflames, move one toward one's full realization. For a greater understanding of this we should recall some facts of theological anthropology about the human cognitive capacity.[1] The most essential and fundamental reality of the person is the love of God, who created us and dwells in us. The presence of this love is guaranteed by the Person of the Holy Spirit. It is on this love that the intellect is grafted in all its dimensions. The intellect works through this love, and through it achieves the final and highest intelligence, which is that of love itself, agape.

Love, in fact, is not just intelligible, it is intelligence. The mind is situated in love and draws vitality from love. The mind is the capacity of inner understanding that includes *reasoning* as an analytic capacity, *intuition* as the capacity for penetrating with a comprehensive gaze, *feeling*, which guarantees the mind's relational dimension, the *affections*, the *will* (whether in its moral or motivational spheres), and even *sensible perception*. All of these dimensions of the mind have been emphasized since pre-Christian antiquity.

From the beginning, Christians saw the usefulness of these dimensions of the mind for the spiritual life. Traditionally, the mind, the *noûs*,[2] has always had this multiple range of registers—from the most natural to what is actually identified with the spirit, that is, with the true capacity of openness to God, to agape. Thus, spiritual awareness came about thanks to the mind understood in this organic totality that plunges into agape. Such totality was traditionally identified with the "heart"—*heart* understood as a complete, articulated human being, who is neither fragmented nor divided.[3]

God Speaks Through
Our Thoughts and Feelings

When it is said that God speaks through our thoughts and feelings, this also means that there are thoughts and feelings through which God does not speak, which can actually derail, confuse, or deceive us. Our thoughts and feelings can, in fact, come from the Holy Spirit, but they also can come from the world, from our environment, from ourselves, or from the devil.

Why is it so important for us to observe which feelings accompany certain thoughts, or from which feelings particular thoughts are born? Because we can have many thoughts, all of which may be good, but they cannot all be followed. The problem is not only to have thoughts centered in the Gospel, but also to know which to dedicate our lives to, which to follow.[4] Thoughts, on the one hand, make up the basic mentality that creates one's orientation—and this is where it is necessary to have good, just thoughts in order to have that healthy spiritual outlook as a background against which to orient one's entire life. On the other hand, however, one's thoughts also make up those views that are the motivation for the guiding options and choices of one's life, including the small, everyday choices. Therefore, one's thoughts both create orientations and lead to specific choices, which have differing degrees of importance.

In and of themselves some thoughts, if followed, exclude other possibilities. It is thus necessary not only to be sure that a thought is good, that it is good for life, but that it is good for *me* and for *my* life. As was mentioned already, we should remember that the Holy Spirit personalizes salvation: the Holy Spirit makes me perceive salvation as present *to me* and *for me*. We can understand also the significance of this spiritual thought experienced in its integrality, namely, how such thoughts also involve my feelings in such a way as to orient me toward love, toward the good, that is, toward the truth, conquering the resistance of sin that is expressed and supported by contrary thoughts and feelings.

The interaction between thoughts and feelings is important, because it allows me to see the state of my personal surrender either to God or to deceptive realities that distance me from God. My feelings betray me, that is, they expose my attachment or detachment to something as well as my motivations. A thought, for example, can be good and in accordance with the Gospel, while the feeling is negative. The question immediately arises: what is it that resists such a thought? What in me does this thought touch in order to provoke such a negative feeling? Or is the feeling negative because my entire being is oriented in this direction? Or still another question: is the thought itself, through a process of purification, making everything negative that exists within me come to the surface, without this indicating a personal attachment to evil?

As can be seen, the reality is very complex. Thoughts can be very abstract and have no relationship to lived experience. Feelings, on the other hand, more easily reveal a person's concrete reality, including his or her memory, making it easier to read his or her thoughts as well. Moreover, thoughts that are in some way also conditioned by culture are not disconnected from feelings, because it is precisely through cultural memory that many attachments are lived out. God, however, always speaks to the actual person and thus speaks through these realities.

Discernment as an Attitude

Discernment has to do with the interaction between thought and feeling. This interaction is a litmus test that indicates the person's orientation. In fact, it is this orientation that determines how one perceives one's thoughts, just as it is because of a particular orientation that particular thoughts arise in the person.

Attention to the interaction between thought and feeling is also useful because it helps to identify the "taste" of one's thoughts and of consciousness itself. All of the great spiritual masters speak of the "taste" or the "flavor" of awareness, and this is exactly the goal of discernment—identifying the "tastes" that accompany spiritual awareness, so that one can exercise this awareness until one has a constant memory of these spiritual flavors and tastes. When one has acquired a certainty of the taste of God and the thoughts that come from him and lead to him, one has come to an attitude of discernment.

> When one has acquired a certainty of the taste of God and the thoughts that come from him and lead to him, one has come to an attitude of discernment.

In fact, all of the exercises of discernment have the goal of acquiring a constant attitude of discernment. There is, therefore, a great difference between discernment as a spiritual exercise within prayer and the attitude of acquired discernment that has already become a *habitus*, the constant attitude and prayerful disposition to which all exercises of prayer lead.[5]

The attitude of discernment is a state of constant attention to God, to the Spirit. It is an experiential certainty that God speaks, that God communicates himself, and that my attention to God is already my radical conversion. It is a lifestyle that pervades everything I am and do. The attitude of discernment is constantly living an *open* relationship. It is a certainty that what counts is fixing my gaze on the Lord, and that I cannot conclude the process of my reasoning about something without allowing for the objective possibility that the Lord might make himself heard—precisely because the Lord is free—and might therefore change me.

The attitude of discernment stops me from being stubborn: it is not possible to lock myself into my "being right," because I am not my epicenter; rather, it is the Lord, whom I recognize as the source from whom everything originates and toward whom everything returns. The attitude of discernment is thus a prayerful expression of faith insofar as I remain in the fundamental attitude of radical recognition that constitutes faith: the absolute Otherness of God the Father, Son, and Holy Spirit, free Persons.

Discernment, therefore, is not a calculation, a deductive logic, or a mechanical technology in which one shrewdly weighs means and ends. It's not a discussion, nor an inquiry of majority opinion. Discernment is prayer, the constant asceticism of renouncing my own will and thoughts, working as if everything depended entirely on me, but leaving everything free. Such an attitude is possible only if one is enraptured in a wave of love, because to accomplish this a radical humility is necessary. Humility is, in fact, the feeling that best guarantees the process of discernment. However, as we well know, humility is like freedom: it is only found in love and is a constant dimension of love, and outside of love it does not exist, in the same way that love without humility is no longer love.

All spiritual wisdom, therefore, is not such without the experience of God's love. The exercise of discernment leads us to this foundational experience of God's love, which can then become a constant, prayerful attitude of discernment, of acquiring the humility that is above all docility, that is, the attitude of "letting speak."

Two Stages of Discernment

The masters distinguish two stages of discernment: a purgative stage that converges toward an authentic self-knowledge in God and of God in one's own history and life, and a second stage in which discernment becomes a *habitus.*

The most authentic experience of God, which permits no doubts, ambiguity, or illusions, is the forgiveness of sins. Only God forgives sins. Only Reconciliation is capable of regenerating us so that we are made "new persons." Therefore, the first phase of discernment moves us toward an ever more radical knowledge of self and of God. This knowledge of self inevitably becomes a recognition of ourselves as sinners. Knowledge of God translates into the knowledge of ourselves as forgiven sinners.

The experience of the hell of sin, of the no-way-out represented by the path of sin, and the encounter with death as the wages of sin, is an authentic dimension of the experience of God as mercy, as absolute love, as gratuitous pardon, regeneration, resurrection, and new creation. The experience of forgiveness, an integral and total experience of the God who is love, becomes that fundamental taste on which the capacity to discern will be based. Memory thus becomes the privileged path of the spiritual life. We progress reminding ourselves of what we are called to be.

Memory is that capacity we must develop with care and attention in order to learn how to discern and acquire a constant attitude of discernment. This does not mean simple recollections or nostalgia, but the memory of God and of his action. It is therefore a memory in which God himself acts. This memory is based on the liturgy, in which memory becomes the eternal *anamnesis* of God in which we are able to see history and things as God remembers them. This does not have to do with my remembering my sins, defects, and shortcomings, but with how the Lord, in his love of these realities of mine, remembers them. Forgiveness occurs within liturgy, and its memory begins in the liturgy and grows, thanks to the liturgy, by that eternal *anamnesis* in which the entire life of a Christian flows into the Holy Spirit.

The discernment that leads to this fundamental event is based on our integral consciousness, which enables us to follow the inspiration and illumination of the Holy Spirit, finally coming to see ourselves with God's eyes, no longer remaining alone in the consideration of our sins. In general, we do recognize our limitations, errors, and even sins. We know how we should act and what we should do, yet we don't do it. And if we do succeed at something, the situation often gets worse because what we see makes us arrogant and increases our inner disintegration. Not only must we know ourselves, but we must acquire, through discernment, that fundamental attitude of dialogue, of openness. It has to do with discovering ourselves *within* a healed relationship, of not finding ourselves alone with our sin, of not promising for the millionth time to become better, which we cannot do by ourselves any more than we can save ourselves.

> [Discernment] has to do with discovering ourselves *within* a healed relationship, of not finding ourselves alone with our sin.

No other person can substitute for God at such deep levels of relationality. No one can heal a sinner except Christ, the Healer, and no one can console an afflicted sinner except the Spirit, the Consoler. Through discernment I reach the threshold of that fundamental, vivifying relationship God has had toward me from the moment of my creation, and which I now relive in the redemption and in Reconciliation, discovering myself as a new creation.

Discernment Does Not Occur in Solitude

It is interesting that the ancient spiritual masters did not write rules for discernment, because they considered discernment to be possible only within discipleship or spiritual direction. Furthermore, one of the goals of spiritual direction was precisely that of teaching discernment. This means that to learn how to discern, it is above all necessary to learn a relationship, to enter into a healthy relationship.

In the West, St. Ignatius of Loyola, for example, who developed very precise rules for discernment, nevertheless indicates that such rules are mainly for the one guiding the exercises to be able to recognize better the movements in the one making the exercises. Consequently, even St. Ignatius holds that the precise rules he worked out can only be used within a spiritual dialogue, therefore within a spiritual relationship. This highlights the fact that our entire spiritual tradition in itself values discernment, but is also aware of the risks of spiritual deviations if discernment is not exercised in the right way.

In Cassian we see that discernment is the virtue that renders every other virtue virtuous. Without discernment, even the most holy reality, even charity, can be illusion and deceit. Ignatius of Loyola also speaks of a discrete *caritas*, that is, of charity with discernment. If discernment is so important, the Fathers must have had a reason for keeping it within an interpersonal pedagogy.

The reason probably lies in the fact that discernment, in spite of maintaining this fundamental human openness, nevertheless leads to a great personal certainty, thus running the risk of a sort of self-sufficiency in understanding what and how one should be and what one should do. Moreover, since we live within a highly technological and rationalistic culture, we are accustomed to organizing and regulating—and therefore to dominating. The risk exists that we will take the rules of discernment as a technique, a sort of method for "understanding" God, for deciphering God's will and thus in some way opening up the possibility for the illusion of possessing God.

Clearly we should understand spiritual dialogue in its authentic sense. It does not mean openness to any friend whatsoever, but to a person who understands the spiritual life, who has experience and is capable of seeing me with a spiritual eye, of seeing how salvation is at work in me, of how my life can be opened to it and can in turn transmit salvation to others and become in this way a life fulfilled.[6]

Two Ancient Examples of Discernment

Repetition is a simple way of verifying the connection between a thought and the rest of one's cognitive capacity. Repetition helps to show the real relationship between a thought and the truth of the person, thus the importance of a thought for the authentic life of a particular person. At this point it is possible to understand why repetition represents one of the most ancient methods of discernment, one that we find often in the Bible as well as in the liturgy. Modern men and women have a certain allergy to repetition, but the ancients greatly appreciated it.

As a way of discernment, in what does this repetition consist? If one repeats the same thought often, one begins to sense within oneself a reaction: it either begins to be pleasurable, warming the heart more and more and releasing its creativity, or else it becomes ever more tedious and foreign to the point that it even begins to be bothersome. We are able to welcome and integrate everything that is true and therefore obtain true life. Even if the thought deals with something dramatic, it can arouse a sense of beauty. Everything that *simulates* truth, however, that pretends to be true but in fact is not, can be fascinating and attractive in the beginning but, after a few repetitions, begins to weaken and even trouble us, making us feel uncomfortable. The contents one writes on a page of a diary, for example, can seem very rich and beautiful. But the truth of this page emerges if it is reread again and again each day for a few weeks, as one erases the words that are no longer perceived as authentic and substitute them with others. Who knows how the contents of this page will seem after several weeks....

Another method the ancients used to test a thought is based on the conviction that the thought to avoid comes from without and is usually accepted either because it has a certain sensory and emotional fascination on the one who considers it a priority, or because it presents itself with such vehemence and insistence that, because of the pressure caused by haste, it is chosen because it is more urgent. The ancient monks advised posing this type of questioning to the thought: "Where do you come from? Do you come from my heart, where the Lord dwells, and are thus my own, or do you come from without and someone else has brought you? Who has brought you? What do you want?" Already by asking these questions one perceives a reaction.

Other questions are also recommended: "Why such urgency? I don't have time for you now." Or "You are forcing me to rush, to undertake this step immediately, but the saints have said that the Holy Spirit as well as the devil want me to be holy; only the devil wants this to happen immediately." To the disciple who asked what sin is, a spiritual master answered: haste.

These "strategies" of spiritual struggle also invite one to listen to a thought that one is not giving much attention to, to focus one's attention on a word of God, on a memory of God, or simply to continue what one is doing. It is precisely with this inner attention, and with a certain disinterest for whatever assails one, that one begins to become aware of the times when a thought does not come from within, when its origins are foreign and its suggestions seem objectifying and moralistic: "you must," "it isn't right," "it's necessary to react," "you must defend," etc.

It is the powerful way in which such thoughts impose themselves, disguised with spiritual, religious, moral, and ethical labels, that contributes immensely to making us forget we are free. Thoughts of this type rob us of our freedom, blinding us to relationships, to the faces of others. They terrorize us with their sense of duty, of urgency, even to the point of disengaging us from love and making us forgetful of our free choice to surrender. The thoughts that impede us from freely surrendering and maintaining a living awareness of ourselves in relationships are thoughts introduced from outside ourselves, not from within. The Holy Spirit does not use the imperative "you must." In the Gospel passage that presents in all its absoluteness the most "programmatic" speech—the Sermon on the Mount—Christ speaks of those who are "blessed." The Gospel is a *revelation*, not a demand; blessed is the one who follows it. Even the Mother of God, at the moment of the Annunciation, did not respond, "Yes, I have to be the Mother of God; otherwise the world will not be saved."

When I do not pay attention to a thought, if the thought is born from the Holy Spirit, it will return because the Lord is humble, and he waits at my door and knocks. When a thought is from the tempter and I do not pay attention, he becomes offended because his is the logic of self-affirmation, and he cannot bear to be ignored. So if I don't pay attention to a thought inspired by the tempter, this thought weakens. But the Christian should prepare for another, more subtle attack. When a thought weighs on me and I resist it by keeping a certain attention in my heart, holding to the memory of God, to an experience of the salvation already felt, to keeping faithful to my task, or to daily life, then the thought is transformed into another thought more conformed to my personal manner of thinking, character, and experience. This makes discernment much more difficult and is more typical of the second stage of discernment and thus will be treated

> The Holy Spirit does not use the imperative "you must." The Gospel is a *revelation*, not a demand; blessed is the one who follows it.

more in depth in Part II. This experience does not happen often to beginners who are tempted in a baser way, or with beautiful thoughts that present themselves with more emphasis or more haste, or who still openly suffer the temptation to sin and vice.

In neither case, however, is it necessary to pay attention to the thought. It is not necessary to be rushed into responding. On the contrary, spiritual tradition actually advises us to mock such thoughts. When we are assailed by doubts, by the negative judgments of others, by violent responses to others, or by thoughts of what others think about us, it does not hurt to step in front of the mirror and have a good laugh in the face of these thoughts, knowing that nothing serious will happen in our lives if we scorn them. If we listen to these thoughts, however, we will soon fall into sin, or at least we will lose our peace of heart because we are worrying about things that in themselves have no weight and do not even exist until we begin to consider them, giving them existence with our attention.

Someone may ask if this does not contradict Jesus' affirmation in Mark 7:20–23 that evil comes from the human heart: "It is what comes out of a person that defiles. For it is from within, from the human heart, that evil intentions come: fornication, theft, murder, adultery, avarice, wickedness, deceit, licentiousness, envy, slander, pride, folly. All these evil things come from within, and they defile a person."

First of all, it is necessary to remember that the context of this discussion is related to clean and unclean foods. Christ shows that it is not eating an unclean food that makes us impure, but that indecency comes from the human heart. The Fathers always understood this verse in the sense that temptation comes from the outside, but because the heart is the organ of decision, of choice, and therefore of surrender, it is in our hearts that we make certain realities our own. When our hearts choose temptation, and therefore sin, they begin to conserve the memory of sin. Then images, memories, impressions, sensations, and thoughts of sin present themselves as if they were our own. The struggle then shifts to the interior.

If we welcome redemption, however, and choose it, renouncing sin, welcoming the Holy Spirit's action, offering all the attention and space in our hearts to the image of God within us, then sin remains buried. This image of God is revealed as God's true action and, in the synergy between us and Holy Spirit, we come to be like God. Such hearts are paradise on earth, the remnant of Eden, the dwelling of God, the temple of the Holy Spirit. So, it can be clearly seen that images, the sinful impressions that arise in us and inhabit our consciences, rather than being something from *within* us, actually pertain to the "old man," the fleshly being that the spiritual being perceives as foreign, impeding us from being free and from living the fruits of the Spirit.

CHAPTER 3

The Dynamics of the First Stage of Discernment[1]

Freeing Ourselves from the Mentality of Sin

THE FIRST STAGE OF DISCERNMENT is the purgative stage. Because purification leads to knowledge, it is a stage of knowledge of self and knowledge of God. In order to be truly realistic—as has already been noted—this knowledge is found in forgiveness and therefore in the salvation that God effects in people. Sin takes place within love because it is only within love that the experience of freedom is possible, and therefore also the free choice not to surrender to God.[2]

In fact, sin means understanding oneself outside of love, having a vision of self disconnected from others. In this vision of sin, the most radical self-recognition is not in extending oneself toward others, but in extending oneself in an egotistical way and also in seeing others from this perspective, even to the point that one sees others only for what they can do for one. Sin cuts off relationships and then perceives them in a perverted way. For example, if before sin one saw the world as the place of encounter with one's Creator, after sin it is perceived only in terms of oneself and how it can serve one.

People dominate the earth with a self-affirming principle even to the point of usurping creation, as with everything else, into the service of their selfishness. Even more serious, however, is the danger that one may see God only in the service of one's selfishness. Sin enlarges the ego, presenting everything that exists as possible capital to reassure it that, divorced from relationships and sensing its existential fragility and its sentence of death, it has a right to help itself to everything possible in order to feed its illusion of being able to assure its own life. But this is precisely an illusion, because the only thing that gives a person life is the very sacrifice of egoism, the death of the self affirming principle, in order to enter into the sphere of love, the only reality that remains and that is therefore eternal.

How is it that sin is capable of alluring people with its delusions? It is so successful because sin creates a mentality. Now, a mentality of sin is not necessarily an anti-God mentality, even though it is necessarily an anti-love mentality, that is, a mentality that convinces people it is not useful to love, insinuates a distrust of loving sacrifice, and fills people with fear when they are faced with dying to themselves by suggesting the weakness and insufficiency of love's arguments until they are frozen when faced with sacrifice. If love is only realized in Christ's way—that is, the paschal way, the way of sacrifice and resurrection—then sin is precisely the denying of the paschal logic and thus the emptying of Christ's redemptive work.

Sin convinces one that Christ's work, that is, his Passion, is not a sufficient argument for one's own passion. This is actually an attack against the Holy Spirit, since the work of the Holy Spirit is the personalization of the Christ-event for each of the baptized. It is the Holy Spirit who makes the salvation won by Christ my Lord *my* salvation. Sin manages to convince me that the Holy Spirit is an illusion and that I can achieve on my own what is necessary to save myself. Sin's greatest deception lies precisely in this: in convincing me that it is enough to *know* what to do to save myself in order to be saved.

> Sin convinces one that Christ's work, his passion, is not a sufficient argument for one's own passion, and yet the work of the Holy Spirit is the personalization of the Christ-event for each of the baptized.

Breaking away from relationships, indifferent to the love of the Holy Spirit who dwells within them, people think they are in a position to love God and to do what they understand should be done. They are only free to act this way, however, because freedom is a constitutive dimension of love. God's love dwells within them without constraining them to live according to the good. It is exactly in this freedom given them in God's presence, experienced as a constitutive element of love, that people can break away from love and project an *imagined* love. Deluded in this way, they believe they are loving because they act according to certain precepts and commandments in their preestablished structure of religious values, which they have substituted for the living God, the God of faces, the God of love.

More Than a Subtle Temptation

The purgative way is full of deceptions and illusions because of this self-affirming principle. One will be continually tempted to confess sins, events, habits, and errors in order to purify oneself. I confess a sin, perhaps am even emotionally moved, and right away I make a firm resolution to act against this sin or to make amends. However, I must be attentive to see if I am dealing with a true resolution, or acting in a hidden way to *merit* forgiveness or salvation. And that is not all. Even this could also be a subtle way of asserting myself, my own will or ego, following a religious, absolutely Gospel-based or heroic resolution that, nonetheless, is something I have proposed and imposed on myself.

In reality, in such a case, no greater knowledge of God has been reached, because my heart has not been warmed by God. Rather I feel displeased because I am not what I should be. I have become so preoccupied with planning how to reach my ideals that there has not arisen within me a passionate love for God, an enthusiasm that is true zeal, not a passion for an idea or for a thing, but for the Lord's Face. There is no contrite heart, broken by the tears that alone express my involvement in Christ's passion, the price of our salvation.[3]

In this first stage of discernment I know how to choose those thoughts that lead to a radical recognition of God: that lead to yielding before God, to admitting that I have chosen myself before God, to recognizing that my true focus has been my ego and not God. The first stage of discernment, in fact, separates my thoughts in two epicenters: my ego and God. This stage deals with my deepest self-knowledge, with how I most deeply recognize myself: whether I perceive myself as the self who thinks, programs, acts, and subscribes to life apart from others, or whether I recognize myself as a person of relationships and ties, who sees myself together with others; above all, in the radical orientation of the relationship that gives life and is the recognition of God in Jesus Christ.

In the first stage, discernment leads us to a sapiential experience of radicalism based on the Gospel: it's either Christ or myself. In reality, the true spiritual question does not present itself in this way, because this antagonism is exactly the consequence of original sin. Here the "ego" is considered as the self-affirming subject that makes itself the center of everything in the sense of St. Paul's understanding of the flesh. The "ego" feels itself fulfilled if it is the focus of everything that exists, that is, of creation and relationships. Herein, however, lies precisely the deception because it means binding things and relationships to a non-vital center that is not the true source.

Instead, if people choose Christ, they choose the things of Christ; that is, everything will call Christ to mind and will lead to him, and they will find themselves with Christ in everything. If they choose themselves, they will become lost in the things through which they seek to save themselves. In fact, forgetting themselves for these "things" will become their tomb.

Discernment means discovering, through our very thoughts and feelings, the movements of the Holy Spirit, to the point that we admit our sin—self-love that puts ourselves at the center of the universe—and not just our peccadilloes. At the same time, discernment is the art of avoiding the traps proposed by humanity's enemy spirit, who wishes people never to reach the true knowledge of God as love but continue to remain alone, centered on themselves, perhaps deluded into believing they believe in God and are following God, notwithstanding the fact that they are actually following themselves, even if they do so under a religious pretext.

We can explain this struggle with an image: a man discovers that snakes have entered his room. After killing them, he thinks he is safe and that he only needs to make sure no more snakes can enter. This is like the person who confesses some sins and thinks that at this point the important thing is not to repeat those acts again. However, this man has forgotten that in a corner, hidden under a cupboard, is the mother of the snakes about to give birth to more snakes, not outside, but inside the room. What does this mean? That until I confess *sin*, my spiritual life will not bear true fruit. It is necessary for me to reach within myself to uproot *my love for my own will*—the mother of all sins—which subtly tricks me into thinking myself to be God, thus grounding my life on and in service of myself.

How Discernment Begins

It is commonly said that one can recognize a spiritual thought by the way it leads to peace and fills one with joy. However, anyone who knows a little about discernment knows that peace, in itself, means nothing. Rather, it is necessary to see what kind of peace it is, and what brought the peace about. Most of all, in order to test the thoughts that accompany the peace, we need to understand where these thoughts lead us and toward what they orient us.

People are extremely sensitive to serenity, joy, and a sort of inner well-being. Perhaps this is why the great spiritual masters began to outline rules of discernment, distinguishing precisely between one kind of peace and another, between one kind of joy and another. Ignatius of Loyola, both in the *Exercises* as well as in his letters or autobiographical texts, is very explicit about the distinctions between two types of joy.

"Bubbly" Joy

The first type of joy is one we can define as "bubbly." It is a very attractive and convincing joy. However, in itself, this joy is precisely the type of feeling in which temptation is sown and in which the Holy Spirit is not at work. Here are a few characteristics of this joy. First—and this is why we have defined it as such—it is just like a "bubbly" drink: when you pour it into a glass, it makes a lot of foam, a lot of noise, but then the foam disappears rapidly and, if one does not drink it right away, in a short time it needs to be thrown out. In the same manner, this type of joy presents itself powerfully, with intense emotions. It is noisy and short-lived. Then, when it goes away, it leaves behind a type of bitterness, like champagne that has been sitting in a glass too long.

Usually, it is obvious what initiated or caused this type of joy; its origins are identifiable. Often it is tied to a place I have visited, to an event I participated in, to someone I have met, a piece of music I have heard, an image I have seen, a success I have had, food I have eaten, a party I went to.... Its source is almost always something external. It's a joy that grows quickly, is very intense, and touches me even on a sensory level. Precisely because it's so noisy, it demands expression: to laugh loudly without cause, to relate immediately what was felt.

When people have experiences of this type, they begin to speak without taking a breath, in a clearly exaggerated manner, impelled by this joy to communicate, to cry out, or to speak in a vehement way. Often young people have told me that they experience this state of joy at parties. It is curious that, in spite of this communicative thrust, they often still feel quite lonely. This joy then leads to thinking only of oneself. The "other" is only useful to me as the receiver of my need to speak. Since others are merely passive listeners, I don't need to pay any real attention to them, enter into a real relationship with them, or give them any recognition. Instead, I truly draw close to others when I pay attention to them, not to their physical beings but to what they *feel*.

The spiritual fathers also warn about the risk of becoming too focused on feelings, pleasures, and joys, even if these come from prayer. This focus on our state of well-being can become so great that we begin to pray only to experience these pleasurable feelings, so much so that we could even forget the Lord while praying, in much the same way that when overflowing with this "bubbly" joy we are more attentive to what we feel than to those with whom we are speaking.

This joy creates an unreal, abstract enthusiasm. Falling prey to this, we think we can do anything, become overconfident, and thoughts come to us that we would normally discard as totally nonsensical. In fact, people often have made mistakes choosing jobs or schools, lifestyles, or marriage partners, precisely because they have made their choices when they were dominated by this kind of joy.

Bubbly joy makes us believe that we can do the impossible because the world it projects is not realistic. It is based on inaccurate knowledge of ourselves. In this "joy," there is not the least space for a realistic gaze, a memory of our illnesses, our mistakes, our failures. We only see the future, replete with images of exaggerated heroism. This short-lasting joy quickly passes, often at a moment's notice, leaving a gaping emptiness inside that must be refilled instantly since it is unpleasant. In fact, after having felt this joy, we can actually feel quite sad.

Hundreds of times young people have told me that they have felt this after going out to a bar. They return home, close their doors, feel incredible emptiness, and become downcast. The same thing can happen even after having finished an intense task that offers a lot of satisfaction. After having rested from such a task, a strange restlessness arises, a not-knowing-what-to-do, accompanied by guilty feelings that perhaps one pushed oneself too far or played the protagonist too much. These are the typical remnants of this "bubbly" joy. Often, people even begin to admonish themselves for something they have done or said, for having laughed so much or having gotten themselves into such a state.

In fact, when we are overtaken by this type of "joy," we don't pace ourselves; we see ourselves in an exaggerated way. Sadness follows, a dull reproach and emptiness that calls into question the moments of joy we have experienced. We may feel ashamed for having done certain things. The emptiness becomes unbearable, and we need to do something to assuage the pain of this emptiness and to silence the little reproaches that rumble within. We need to draw attention away from the interior world.

It is often at this point that people turn on the radio or the TV, go to the fridge to get something to eat, or even use sex or drugs as compensation. Many vices and difficulties have their roots in these moments of emptiness. Unconsciously, they are using compensations to try to arouse again the feeling of intense joy that they experienced. In these moments, one suddenly feels the need to go out, take a walk, make a call; but actually nothing really satisfies one, and one ends up deciding to return to the same experience, in the company of the same people in which one felt this "bubbly" joy.

Many young people have told me that they live for Saturdays, knowing that on Saturday they will be going out again, searching for the same feelings. Yet even this only appeases someone a few times. Afterward, a person cannot be satisfied any longer by doing the same things, because the joy is no longer as intense. So the person needs to heighten the excitement. An ever-stronger stimulus is needed. He or she becomes more daring in order to satisfy this uncontrollable desire for whatever is new and different. Eventually, a person can become dependent on actually creating excitement to mask the emptiness.

This is the logic behind almost all escapism today, from the apparently insignificant and innocuous to actual depravity. In this sense, a large part of our culture's problem is actually spiritual. The cure and prevention that come from the psychological and socio-logical fields, even if useful, are certainly not exhaustive; they need to be completed with the art of spiritual struggle. If de Lubac maintains that the problem of the great thinkers of the modern age was not simply a philsophical or intellectual problem but a spiritual one, the same could be said of escapism today, which can be seen as a problem of the spiritual life.

> A person can become dependent on actually creating excitement to mask the emptiness...the logic behind almost all escapism today.

Silent Joy

The second type of joy is silent and humble. It is like water gushing from the earth. All at once we realize we are filled with joy. We don't know where it came from, but it is there. It could happen that we are going along and all at once we feel serene, the faces we encounter appear beautiful, the way seems easy, and no evil thought darkens our minds. Even more, we feel more good-hearted toward others.

Usually, we cannot precisely determine the origin of such joy. It is very difficult to connect it to something external, because deep down we know that this silent joy depends on nothing outside itself for its existence. It could be awakened by something around us, but it is not dependent on it. What triggers it does not give it birth. Instead, this joy seems to belong to us, to be carried deep within us. It gushes forth unexpectedly and cannot be controlled or commanded. Unpredictably, it makes itself felt.

This joy is very composed and peaceful, a joy that moves elegantly, slowly, and simply. Its unmistakable characteristic is that it illumines everything, making things clear and beautiful. It is a joy that erases shadows and evil. It shows forth the utter transparency of all things, lifting them above the level of mere possession. It is joy that arouses contemplation. Under the influence of silent joy, it becomes easy to remember God. When we are penetrated by this joy, we no longer desire even what most pleases us. We no longer need to possess these things, storing them up and attaching ourselves to them. We no longer try to possess people. We feel in communion with everyone. We don't need to express this joy as soon as we feel it. Rather, because it makes us feel that we are in communion with others, this joy often needs no expression at all, or at least no noisy communication. We feel as if communication is already taking place, and we sense that the moment will come when it will be right to speak, entrusting things to others naturally.

When filled with this joy, one's fear disappears, concerns are distanced, and worries have less power, even if they cannot be entirely smoothed away. The stronger the joy, the less one feels the need to express it. It might seem a contradiction, but this is how it is. The further along the spiritual path one is, the less one feels the need to speak about it. This is why beginners speak so much about their experiences, while those who are more advanced say so little. There is no need. This is not because such persons are closed, but because they cannot see what there might be to say. After the powerful experience of a retreat or pilgrimage, beginners often want to speak about what they felt, while those who are more advanced along the spiritual path are persons of few words. Nevertheless, if someone asks them, they are able to speak of themselves without any difficulty.

When we communicate under the influence of this joy, we speak as if we have been entrusted with something precious. Our tone of voice changes as when we are truly praying. We speak with attentiveness so as not to destroy what is so fragile and precious, not to encroach upon the other who is present and to whom we want to give attention. Silent joy urges us to a greater respect for others and for ourselves. Thoughts born of authentic joy are respectful and optimistic. Even if the tasks before us are difficult to do, we have quiet confidence; we are both realistic and optimistic. Though aware of difficulties, we are nonetheless ready to go ahead. Silent joy is longer-lasting than bubbly joy. It can well up within us for hours, days, even months. We may remain in a very peaceful and even beautiful state month after month. Our work and our relationships go well, even if perhaps just a year ago we were fighting with everyone.

It is possible to remain under this influence, as under the "covering" of the Holy Spirit, for a long time. When this joy seems to disappear—if we live through something very violent, it can disappear unexpectedly—it is still actually within us. It is similar to the ground-water on a limestone plateau that disappears underground for a while and then, all at once, reappears. Sooner or later this joy resurfaces, because it is part of us. This certainty is very beautiful. Even more, the *conviction* that it will return is so strong that recalling it when the joy seems to have disappeared can be enough to make it resurface anew. If we are able to remember how the joy felt, what thoughts and attitudes accompanied it, or where we were when it last flowed freely, then often the joy will be felt again.

The philokalic Fathers called this "sobriety": being sober and vigilant, staying focused on realities that are already tasted and secure and moving on from there, seeking traces of this joy in whatever we encounter. In a certain sense, this joy can be safeguarded. We do not have to return to precise experiences or special places to feel it. We carry it within ourselves, and it belongs to us.

Following are some characteristics of this spiritual joy. When we experience spiritual joy, the thoughts that come to us could be truly spiritual, while in the state of bubbly joy the thoughts that come to us are certainly not. Silent joy is the sphere in which the Holy Spirit most often speaks to us.

Silent joy is the sphere in which the Holy Spirit most often speaks to us.

The great spiritual masters began discernment precisely by identifying the characteristics of their various feelings. Ignatius of Loyola, for example, experienced this when, after having been wounded during the siege of Pamplona, he underwent a long convalescence at home. He began his discovery of discernment precisely by identifying the two types of joy described earlier and that are found, even if in other terms, in all Ignatian literature.

In his *Autobiography*, Ignatius describes himself as a "man devoted to the world's vanities." Confined to bed, he read the chivalrous novels of the age and his head swelled as he imagined himself in the role of one or the other protagonist, winning the most beautiful women in all of Spain, a champion in the feats that he would have carried out in their service. Carried away by these thoughts, he was always happy, and they absorbed him for hours without his even noticing. When he finished reading all the novels in the house, however, he was given a book on the life of Christ and one on the stories of the saints. Seeing that there was nothing else to read, Ignatius had to content himself with these.

Given that he had the habit of always picturing himself as the hero, when Ignatius read the lives of the saints he identified with St. Francis and St. Dominic. He stopped to think that if St. Francis or St. Dominic had done this or that, then surely he should do the same. Then, beginning to reflect on what he had read, thinking of the chivalrous novels and the saints, he began to notice two different types of joy: one that gave him happiness but, when it abandoned him, left him feeling dry and discontent, and the other that not only gave him consolation—not euphoria—but on dissipating also left him happy and content. Marveling at this difference, Ignatius began to reflect and to understand the different spirits that stirred in him and that he later discovered to be from two different sources: one from the devil and the other from God.

The Fundamental Rule

Let us now consider the main rule of discernment in the primary stage, the rule that will orient us in the right direction so that our relationships with God will continuously deepen. This process, as has already been pointed out, will end with a real encounter of forgiveness.

Discernment moves along the borders between psychology and spirituality. It has to do with understanding what within one's world is from God and how God communicates himself to one. Thus, discernment, on one hand, deals with a purely psychological sphere—such as observing feelings, thoughts, and changes in one's state of being—and, on the other hand, with disclosing the spiritual dimension of these realities.

This first rule considers one's state of peace. At the psychological level, one experiences peace when one's thoughts and feelings are oriented toward the same object. When, on the contrary, one is emotionally oriented toward one thing and rationally focused on another, one feels restless, disturbed, desolate, dejected, and so forth. One's orientation is no longer integrated and whole because, with one's reason and one's sentiment oriented in different directions, one is torn between two different objects.

Another important question arises: how do I know what I am oriented toward, since feeling at peace is not enough to be sure that I am directed toward the right object? It is easy to find people who, aware of their feelings, experience peace, and from this they deduce that the objects toward which they are oriented are good. Psychologically the distinction between the peace that accompanies someone oriented in the right direction and the peace that accompanies someone oriented in the wrong direction is not so immediately obvious. This is precisely why discernment is so necessary and why it is not so easy.

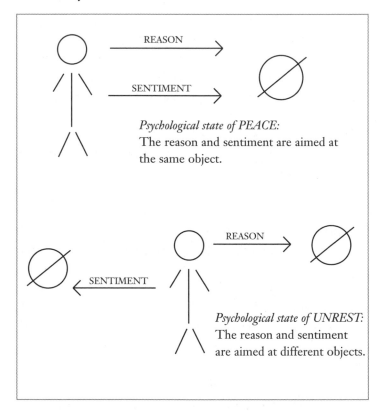

Psychological state of PEACE:
The reason and sentiment are aimed at the same object.

Psychological state of UNREST:
The reason and sentiment are aimed at different objects.

As we can see, it is not so important to concentrate on how and what we feel, but rather on where these feelings come from and where they lead, and toward what the thoughts that come from these feelings propel us. Under the influence of psychology, in spiritual formation today there is a risk that the art of discernment will be lost because the spiritual struggle is being avoided. As soon as someone begins to feel badly, various psychological means are instantly applied to help that person get out of a mood and to feel better. There is always someone around to rescue others from feeling badly. Suggestions are instantly at hand: change work schedules, the environment, the people in the community, etc. However, such psychologically informed coping mechanisms cancel out the possibility of a "spiritual reading" of a struggling person's day, his or her history, or even life.

Instead, it is much more important to explore the thoughts that arise during personal struggles and understand toward what these thoughts orient us. If we did this, we might be surprised to discover that a certain uneasy, sad, restless state of being is aroused by the action of the Holy Spirit. We will see more about this later. But if we do not accept that our spiritual lives might also have moments perhaps quite long moments—of unease, the Holy Spirit's action eludes us and in the end, God can say nothing to us.

> If we do not accept that our spiritual lives might have moments of unease...the Holy Spirit's action eludes us and in the end, God can say nothing to us.

Since, in the first stage of discernment, we are focused on only two "objects"—self and God—it is easy enough to decipher that these objects reveal themselves in particular thoughts arising from a state of being. The questions we ask ourselves have a clear yes or no answer: "Are these thoughts moving me toward God, a more mature openness, and a more practical love? Or are they leading me increasingly to close myself off from others, to reassure myself, always to defend myself more, and to fulfill myself according to my own will?" However, it is necessary to be attentive and not to be deceived by immediate impressions. In daily life, all of us are aware of moments of selfishness, when we look out only for ourselves. There are also moments when we do things with love and for love, for God and for others. One should not allow oneself to be deceived by impressions and conclude one's fundamental orientation from a few actions. Rather, one must fix one's gaze below the surface, where one experiences inner unity in the deepest part of one's being, a place deeper than psychological states or ethical choices.

There, in the deepest part of our beings, we embrace salvation, adhere to our baptisms, cling to Christ with all our hearts, although in our day-to-day lives we stumble and sin. It is a totally different matter if, in our most profound reality, we remain anchored in ourselves, fully preoccupied with ourselves, and only superficially wanting to act like new persons in day-to-day life. Grapes cannot be picked from thorns, and the fruits, actions, and way of thinking of a new person cannot be expected from someone whose heart has remained centered on itself.

The Action of the Enemy Spirit on the Person Who Is Oriented Toward Self

Let's try to understand this dynamic with an example. Fundamentally, let us say, we are centered on ourselves, that is, still seeking ourselves. Perhaps in our daily actions we can hide behind nice, religious, holy gestures, but still we must admit a fundamental attachment to our own wills that we cannot shake. In this case, what will human nature's enemy spirit—as St. Ignatius calls it—try to do? Try to keep reason and sentiment united. To what end? The enemy's goal is to keep us feeling good about ourselves, to keep us at a certain level of peace, and to keep us moving along the wrong path.

In this case, the tempter mainly acts on the emotions. He feeds the senses with sensuality, with consolations and sensual pleasures. When I say "sensual," I mean those base, petty, and mean inclinations, such as the preoccupation with how I should act so that people will accept me, so that I am applauded, so that I have a warm house, a soft bed, good food, glory, praise, health, a nice car, power, etc. Such inclinations are mainly directed toward the reassurance of not having worries or difficulties, of feeling "fine."

What does the enemy do to my reason while nourishing my emotional side? He fills my mind with a thousand reasonable excuses to prove to myself and others that I am on the right path. The Greek Fathers even had a word to describe this game: the so-called *dikaioma*, the attempt I make to justify myself with whatever word I can find from Scripture, from the rule, or from spiritual authors in order to give myself the illusion of being on the right path.

Acting in this way upon my mind, the enemy tries to give reasons and to confirm what he makes me feel emotionally, that is, he supplies me with motivations for being centered on myself. Such motivations often depend on the culture I come from, on my character, and on my personal history. It is not easy to dismantle these motivations, because a million reasons can be found to justify the attitudes underlying them, hiding the base aspect of sensual pleasure.

The Action of the Holy Spirit on the Person Who Is Oriented Toward Self

What does the Holy Spirit do instead, when the person is self-oriented? He seeks to *separate* reason and emotion, thus provoking restlessness and uneasiness in the person. To what end? The goal is that the person might stop, reflect, and change his or her orientation. The Holy Spirit mainly acts on the reason. When one's reason begins to break off from the direction toward which it has been headed and orient itself instead toward God, one begins to feel uncomfortable, because the emotional and rational components are not turned to the same object. This is why moments of uneasiness, of a troubled, struggling soul, are necessary in the spiritual life.

When we are oriented toward ourselves, the Holy Spirit cannot act on our sentiments because they are busy with sensual pleasures. The Holy Spirit cannot act because the sentiments are not open to any "bait." Our senses swell with sensual pleasures. When we are satisfied with sensual pleasures, we are unable to consider spiritual ones. Without these moments of indisposition caused by the Holy Spirit acting on our reason, there is no conversion. It is when we are forced to abandon positions of pleasure, the straws from which we suck in pleasures, that we begin to see clearly that we are spiritually unwell.

Since the Holy Spirit cannot work on our feelings, he suggests *arguments* to make us confront the fact that we are focused on our own navels. As a consequence, we begin to feel bad, to feel down in the dumps, disturbed and restless. As an aside, how delicate pastoral work must be to respect the nature of the spiritual life. Pastoral ministers can easily fall into two errors. First, they can try to touch the person's emotions in order to attract him or her to the life of the Gospel. They do not realize, however, how difficult it is to compete with the culture of entertainment, and they risk having people respond to the Gospel out of a desire for companionship, without obtaining true, mature, long-lasting conversions. Second, pastoral activity risks being reduced to a mere discourse on values that is more or less interchangeable with that of civil society. Instead of pastoral ministry putting pressure on the emotions, as in the case above, pastoral outreach becomes detached, rational, and moralistic.

So what can be done if a person's feelings are caught up in powerful sensual pleasures and the person is still likewise rationally oriented? It is useless to say, "If you accept Christ, you will have peace, joy, and life." It would be like offering a menu from an elegant restaurant to someone who is full from eating junk food. The person is not ready to leave anything behind because the pleasure, no matter how poor, still exists. *Who knows if I will really find what is promised...?* This is why the Holy Spirit acts, instead, on our reason, for we can more easily be attracted by a new, different thought.

If the reason is presented with the logic and the thought of the Gospel, it can be "tempted" to listen. As soon as one's reason attends to the thoughts inspired by the Gospel, it is illumined with brief flashes of light that show with impressive clarity and lucidity that this is the way to true life, while the former path had not been the right one. It is as if in a profound way, more intuitive than rational, one's reason understands that the Gospel is true, that things truly are the way the Gospel says they are. As soon as reason is stopped short by the Gospel with the inner—even if brief—conviction that the Gospel has meaning and is true, then one's sentiments begin to weep terribly and break out in a frightened cry, dreading having to leave all their pleasurable attachments behind. But as soon as the person starts to feel bad, his or her former reasoning quickly reasserts itself, reinstating his or her preoccupation with the self. The person "refinds" himself or herself and feels "good" again.

This situation is also typical of certain pastoral approaches, retreats, and spiritual experiences. As soon as the Word begins to engrave itself upon us, we become frightened by what is happening and leave things as they are, so that we can keep going on with our lives unchanged. The Holy Spirit, however, acting on the reason through these brief, obvious flashes, continues to provoke spiritual *dis*-ease and restlessness, almost biting our consciences with the clarity of reason. If we continue to feel badly for a while, then it is possible that our sentiments can be moved for an instant toward the Gospel that reason has begun to consider. If this happens, we find ourselves in a new situation: at least for brief instants, both rationally as well as emotionally, we are oriented *toward* the Gospel, toward God. We have already defined the experience of peace as this integral orientation of thoughts and feelings in the same direction. We then experience peace just as we had before, but a different kind of peace. Only now can we fully appreciate the difference between these two types of peace. We can hear this difference explained a million times over, but we cannot truly understand it without experiencing it ourselves.

It is only after I've experienced the difference between being pleased and being happy, being satisfied and being serene, being excited and being joyful that I truly begin to discern. The feeling of consolation I experience when, for an instant, my feelings adhere to the new orientation and are in harmony with a new insight from the Gospel, is often the consolation of a sweet sadness that is very different from what was experienced shortly before, when my feelings were crying out for fear of losing their attachments. Truly consoled, it is now possible for me to shed tears, to cry for my mistaken life as well as for the shocking strength of God's love that has reached me in order to save me.

> It is only after I've experienced the difference between being pleased and being happy, being satisfied and being serene, being excited and being joyful that I truly begin to discern.

The tense happiness we feel through tears—unable to control our emotions, yet filled with joy—is a most intimate consolation. These brief flashes of spiritual consolation become the criteria helping us to welcome the new peace and, in doing so, to begin breaking away from the old peace that is now understood *and* felt to be false. Spiritual emotion fills our hearts in a more incomparable way than any other sensual satisfaction. It becomes that strength on which our wills also find leverage for a complete adherence to God. The feeling that begins to taste the consolation of authentic love has a totally new flavor. It is deeply moved by the drama of God reaching out to us in love. Only the Savior's passion consoles the person God touches and becomes the leverage that makes possible a grateful, free surrender. Without it, abandoning oneself to God runs the risk of being ideological, not personal.

The Action of the Holy Spirit on the Person Who Is Oriented Toward God

Now let us take St. Ignatius' second rule. Imagining a person who is deeply oriented toward God, let us first consider the action of the Holy Spirit. What will the Spirit of God seek to do in this person? The Holy Spirit's goal is to maintain the attraction of a person's reason and feelings toward God, so that the person does not change direction. In order to do this, the Holy Spirit will nurture this person's feelings and care for them so that he or she has the nourishment necessary to live as a believer. When Christians only believe at the level of an ideal, it easily happens that their thoughts are very elevated, structured, even profound, but without "flavor," detached from the heart's feeling. As a result, they suffer from a kind of dualism, defending doctrines with their heads in an austere, even severe way, while their feelings or senses are immersed in the world's sensuality.

When we are seriously oriented toward God, the Holy Spirit nurtures the sentiment with spiritual consolation. This consolation, unlike sensual consolation, is a bit like that second joy that we described earlier, a joy in which everything seems beautiful, our relationship with the Lord is easy, things do not attract us for themselves or for their possession but remind us of God and lead us to praise him, filling us with gratitude. This is not a consolation that comes in solitude; it is true that it is we ourselves who are in consolation, but together with all of reality, we are open to the Creator, in the ease of being bound to God.

Actually, this consolation of the Holy Spirit is identifiable by the very fact that I am not at the center, but in the presence of the Other, of God, with whom I perceive myself to be in a real relationship, in reciprocal belonging. It is a resting in my very Creator. In drawing close to the Lord my love is enflamed. I feel lifted up and attracted by the things that I know will not deceive me but that will remain. Hope grows, and even if I see my own weakness or my very sinfulness, the certainty of salvation is stronger. Even more, I am capable of crying, of being deeply moved because of the salvation given to me by my Lord.

In this situation of spiritual consolation, how does the Holy Spirit act on the reason? In the same way that the enemy of human nature acts on those who are oriented toward themselves: by seeking to supply reasons for what is being felt. In this sense, tradition, the Church, and the lives of the saints are very important, because God uses them to reinforce one's thinking, so that one might know what one is feeling and why one is feeling it. In this way, reason and sentiment move in the same direction, have the same orientation, and create an integral unity within the person.

The Action of the Enemy Spirit on the Person Who Is Oriented Toward God

How does the enemy spirit act on the person who is profoundly oriented toward God? He seeks to tear reason away from sentiment, in such a way that the person's equilibrium is upset, so that the sentiment remains oriented in one direction while reason begins to wander elsewhere and leaves the person feeling restless. The enemy mainly acts on reason, raising false reasoning, creating or increasing impediments, and enlarging obstacles and fatigue.

> How can we recognize false reasoning? By the fact that it always ends up in a preoccupation of how *I* will be, of what *I* will do, by the fact that it leads to a preoccupation with *myself*.

How can we recognize this false reasoning? By the fact that it always ends up in a preoccupation of how *I* will be, of what *I* will do, by the fact that it leads to a preoccupation with *myself*. We can meditate even on the Trinity, but if in this meditation false reasoning inserts itself, then it will lead to worrying about ourselves, of what will become of us, or what people will say, or how many difficulties await us.... Or else, if we meditate on Holy Scripture, then reasons will arise that lead to discrediting the Word of God, to doubts about whether it is truly authentic or if it is necessary to take it seriously, etc. Normally, false reasoning is discovered by the fears that it sows in our souls, fears more or less characterized by a dread of what can happen to us.

In general, the enemy's strategy is to seek to attract the reason by initially posing one or two questions, one or two novel points from the previous spiritual thought. This often happens even in a shocking way, all at once, in the sense that we tell ourselves: "But look, I never considered this before. I was deluded. I didn't check out all the possibilities," and so on. The temptation is complete, however, because the mind has already begun to worry about those things that temptation has aroused.

Often these initial impulses are introduced to our minds when we have let our thoughts wander distractedly here and there in empty memories, recalling people and events from the past. As soon as we begin to worry about such thoughts, introduced by the enemy, we begin to feel badly, becoming restless and disturbed. As a result, the spiritual consolation that previously had given our feelings a taste for the spiritual, even to think spiritually—all this disappears.

At this point the enemy will try to aggravate our unease, frightening us even more. Or he will try to remove the consoling flavor and taste we had felt in the state of spiritual peace that existed before the temptations began, causing us to suffer this disquieting emptiness to an even greater extent. As a consequence, we will be even more eager for consolation and peace, of once more being in a pleasant state. At this point, the enemy has the possibility of proposing a consolation on the feeling level, a sensual consolation. Since we are already feeling so terribly, we allow our thoughts to sink deeper into a patch of quicksand in the vortex of fears and worries, locked within the isolation of the self. It is then that we can give in to sensual temptation and actually experience it as consolation. Temptation, for brief moments, can even move the attention of our sentiments in the direction of the false reasoning that is swaying our intellect. We feel once more a certain peace, because our feelings and thoughts are moving in the same direction—but in the wrong direction. In fact, the consolation is sensual, and we are orientated once more in search of ourselves.

Prayer That Leads to Discernment

Every prayer, if it is authentic, is true prayer, but not every prayer leads to discernment. In order for prayer to lead to discernment, it is necessary to be attentive when one has finished praying to what happened in one's prayer. In other words, to prepare oneself for discernment, it is above all necessary to be attentive to the examination of one's prayer. The masters of discernment always insisted that this examination even be written out. It is from this examination of prayer that one gathers the "stuff" for discernment.

To pray, it is generally recommended that one contemplate a verse from Scripture, a genuinely spiritual text, or a spiritual image. At the time of prayer, the person can proceed along as follows. I have drawn the following six points from some indications of St. Ignatius of Loyola, from Origen, and from some of the philokalic Fathers. At first glance this may seem too restrictive a method, but in reality these points correspond to the dialogical structure in which every interpersonal encounter takes place.

1. Choosing the Place of Prayer, Physical Attitude, and Posture

It is important to choose your place of prayer carefully, because changing places afterward can lead to more distractions. Even when traveling, establish a particular space in which to move, since every novelty becomes a greater temptation for distraction. The position of the body in prayer is also important because it can promote or hinder inner dialogue. In his treatise on prayer, Origen said that the preparatory gestures (such as washing oneself, for example) predispose one to the act that one is about to carry out. They highlight the importance of what one is preparing for and involve the body and senses in the prayer. Added to that, for us Christians, the Holy Spirit dwells within us as our living principle, penetrating us through his action in not only the spiritual and psychological world, but also the corporeal world.

Furthermore, Christian tradition teaches that when the Holy Spirit is active and we labor spiritually, even our psyches and bodies participate in this activity. The same thing happens at a psychological level. Think of a sporting event in which you are rooting for your favorite athlete. When it is his or her turn, you get involved in the game not only emotionally, but also physically. This physical movement is instinctive because your psychological attention is so powerful that it totally absorbs you. The body simply follows.

In the same way, according to Theophan the Recluse, when inner prayer is very intense, the psyche and also the body participate. It could happen that, in a time of authentic and deeply meaningful prayer, you discover you have assumed a particular position. The next time you go to pray, you might choose the same posture associated with that prayer experience. In so doing, you may discover that you are already disposed for profound prayer.

The philokalic Fathers, however, insisted that regardless of how important these suggestions for prayer positions might be, we should not *definitively* prescribe the body's position. If we are too rigid on this point, we risk making posture more important than the prayer itself. In such a case prayer could become only an exercise of will, of concentration, of resistance. It is necessary always to keep in mind as a guiding criteria that prayer is the participation in the life of God, in the Holy Spirit, a coming to an awareness of one's divine relationship as a child in the Son. Thus one should assume positions in prayer that truly facilitate one's inner attention and avoid those that could make one tired or drowsy.

As Christians, as I have already underlined many times, we know that it is the Holy Spirit who is our living principle. It is from the Holy Spirit that life, love, and the light of knowledge come. It is not through physical position, psychic concentration, repeated thoughts, words, or names that we break through the ontological abyss separating us from God and come to true prayer.

2. Where Am I Going? What Do I Want and Desire in This Moment of Prayer?

The answer to the first question is always the same: I am going to pray; I am going into my heart in order to be with the Lord. With regard to the second question, I would recommend writing out the answer.

As you begin a period of prayer, choose a biblical verse, a spiritual text, a spiritual image, an exhortation, a homily, something you believe useful for your relationship with God and for your fuller surrender to his mission in the world.... In other words, choose that which is helpful to your salvation. The spiritual masters advise us to prepare the theme of our prayer the day before, or at least a few hours before. Ignatius of Loyola suggests doing this at night before going to bed. After reading through the selected material, concentrate on one point you consider important enough to devote an hour of prayer to. Express it in a dialogical manner. Here is an example. For an hour of prayer I take the Gospel verse of the healing of the blind man of Jericho (Mk 10:46–52). After having read it, I feel particularly touched by the fact that the man, while still blind, rushed toward Christ who called him. Then I write: "Lord, I ask you, who want and know what is good for me, to give me the grace to experience this strength of faith, this trust that the blind man had in you."

Formulating what you want to ask in prayer is important: humans are reasonable beings, and it is very effective and integral that you know the scope and sense of each action you are about to undertake. By concentrating on what you want to ask, you orient your whole being toward this prayer, and everything that you are begins to be prepared to receive light, illumination, and any gift relative to what you are about to ask.

3. Absolute Prayer (from ab-solutus, not bound)

At this point, I pray to God that I might be freed from attachment to what I have asked for in the preceding step.

Only God really knows what I need in order to relate more wholly to him. So, if the Lord knows that it is better for me, in my relationship with him, that I not taste the thing desired, I ask him not to give it to me.

God always comes in prayer and God always speaks. In order to recognize and accept God, however, I should not preestablish the manner of his coming, what he will say to me, how he will make himself heard, or what I will feel. Let us remember that for centuries humanity awaited the God-Messiah, predetermining when he would come, how he would come, what he would do.... Then he came, but not in the way expected, and people didn't recognize him. They refused him.

Origen emphasizes that the prayer of the Christian is the prayer of the Holy Spirit. In us, it is the Holy Spirit who is truly praying. When my prayer is mature, it adheres to what the Holy Spirit is desiring in me. God the Father listens to the prayer of the Holy Spirit because the Holy Spirit asks what is necessary for my salvation. Therefore, it is actually to my benefit that the Father fulfills the Holy Spirit's prayer, and that I learn, step by step, to bring my prayer in line with that of the Holy Spirit.

This third point is very important for beginners, because it is a reminder not to be attached to the effects of prayer, but to acquire an attitude of detachment, of freedom, of openness, of knowing ever more radically that the Lord listens to prayer, but according to the interpretation that the Holy Spirit gives it. We know that we cannot control, dominate, or manipulate God's coming, the manner of God's grace, or the feelings, states of being, or thoughts that God arouses. God is free, and prayer helps us become ready for an encounter with a free Person.

Note: With these first three points you already enter into dialogue with God. A relationship is established. A conversation is born that helps you to assume that attitude of radical recognition of God as a free Person, who also awakens in you the same freedom typical of a humble love that demands nothing.

These three points should take no more than five minutes.

4. The Nucleus of Prayer

As I enter into this stage of prayer, I seek to bring my thought down into my heart. I do this by listening attentively to my heartbeat for a moment, remembering there the "taste" of a previous encounter with God, trying to put my attention on the Lord. I thus bring into my awareness one of my more "flavorful" previous prayer experiences. At the same time I ask for the gift of the Holy Spirit.

Taking up the text chosen for prayer, I renew in myself the awareness that this Word is full of the Holy Spirit, and I begin to read it with an attitude of respect and deep affinity toward it. I read and reread the text until my inner attention lingers on no more than specific words, drawing a certain pleasure and warmth from them, or until I perceive that some words begin to relate to me more vividly than others. Or else I read the text until I understand certain words as being particularly important to me, to my situation, my ecclesial community, or even to today's circumstances.

Then I focus on and begin to repeat the words in a low voice, aware of my heart and my rapport to this Word that is a Person who speaks to me. Repeating these holy words for several minutes, perhaps with my eyes closed, I am not so attentive to their specific meaning as to *whom they come from, of what they are full,* and *where they want to lead me.* This has to do with the Word of God arousing a veneration, a trembling, a respect in me.

As Origen taught, it is a word that is immersed in the Holy Spirit. When I listen to the word, repeat it, or am simply attentive to it, it is the Holy Spirit that acts in me. The relationship established with the Word is made real by and in the Holy Spirit. It is the Holy Spirit that opens me to the necessary attitude so that the Word might speak to me. Since the Word is a living Person, I do not need to attack it with my ideas or my preconceived notions in order to understand it, but I should rather assume the humble and welcoming attitude that predisposes me so that the Other might reveal himself. When the relationship between the Word and me is the relationship between the lover and the Beloved of the Song of Songs, then mysteries are unveiled.

> When the relationship between the Word and me is the relationship between the lover and the Beloved of the Song of Songs, then mysteries are unveiled.

Every so often (that is, every five or ten minutes), I can linger for a moment to see what this repeated word has aroused in my heart, what feeling it gives birth to, and even what thoughts accompany it. (I can also write down this thought or feeling with a single word in a notebook.)

At times, I interrupt the repetition of the word to speak to the Lord of some reflection or feeling I am experiencing at that moment. The important thing is that the entire time I maintain an attitude of speaking, thinking, and praying to a Thou, that is, that I maintain an attitude of relationship with God. There is no need to be afraid of sharing—perhaps even in a low voice at the beginning—my reflections, questions, gratefulness, and petitions with the Lord, calling the Lord by name.

Sometimes I return to the point formulated for prayer and, while I reread it, try to see it together with one of the words read in Scripture. I try to find the relationship that exists between the formulated point and the Word of God, thus transforming the point into a prayer narrated to the Lord.

The goal to reach in this fourth moment is to hold the word in one's heart and to "cultivate" one's heart in this word. Therefore it is important that someone who prays enters ever more completely into the relationship that the word seeks to establish with that person. Thus is born a dialogue, a conversation with the Word.

Note that distractions and temptations simply need to be included in prayer, referring them to the Lord. It does not help—during prayer, or even in life—to dismiss temptations and distractions, because temptation normally works in the same way as a dog: the more forcefully you try to keep it away, the more it gets angry and bites. Temptation is warded off either by not paying any heed to it or by opening up to the Lord, telling him to listen to the thoughts I am having, to come and assist me, to be with me. As soon as I pray this way and tell the Lord my temptations, I become aware that the temptation goes away; it becomes weaker, draws away, and vanishes. However, it is useful to note the temptations or distractions that are particularly powerful or insistent.

This fourth point should last about 45 minutes.

5. *Thanksgiving and Dialogue with a Saint*

I thank the Lord for this hour of prayer and for everything that has happened. I end the prayer by saying an Our Father, noting that these are the same words that the Lord prayed. I have a short dialogue with a saint, a conversation or simply a remembrance.

It is very important to believe that you are not alone on this path toward the Lord. You are not the only one to suffer, nor do you suffer the most. This social consensus is so important. We seek the company of those who think and act like us. In fact, as relational and social beings, we grow by means of this consensus. This holds true in both positive and negative situations. An unfaithful husband will seek the company of other like-minded men so that he feels justified in his infidelity. It would be much more difficult for him to be in the company of husbands who are faithful to their wives. It is the same with a student who has not passed an exam and who returns home telling his parents about all his friends who, like him, also failed.

From the beginning, Christians have perceived that the natural Adam lives in each person of the human race. It is on the basis of this unity of the human race that it is possible to see why we have all sinned in Adam and why we are all saved in the new Adam. This ontological solidarity is expressed by the Church, the sign and instrument of the unity of the entire human race, as the Council defines it. In the Church, the living memory of the saints is joined to their real participation in our lives. Continually relating to them, we are always in "good company."

Therefore, we have also from a psychological point of view a constructive and positive relational social consensus that can truly help us progress along the path toward the Lord. In a certain sense, the modern age, with its emphasis on only what can be proven empirically, has made us forget this dimension of the Communion of Saints. Along with respect for the deceased, it is really part of the same thing: participation in the Church as a synchronized meeting of the saved of all generations, in which relationships exist beyond the boundaries of time. Faith clearly reveals that death does not put an end to our relationships, but instead, with the saints, the relationships become even stronger.

If the saints already loved so much during the course of their lives, then how much more do they love when they have been glorified in Christ and Christ is glorified in them? This moment of thanksgiving helps us to become aware that we are not metaphorically the body of Christ, but truly Christ's body and as such we live fully in relationship with all those who are members of Christ, disposing us to accept their help. So it is important for the spiritual life for each of us to have at least one friend among the saints upon whom to call and through whom to grow in this awareness.

The saints are not simply models to imitate, which could easily become moralism and psychological depersonalization. The saints are, above all, spiritual inspirations that reach us through these relationships, through the Church, through the liturgy.... In this ecclesial fabric, in this spiritual friendship, an initial inspiration can grow and develop, while the saints make intercession and truly help us. Having friends among the saints is also important if we are to nourish our spiritual imaginations and keep them healthy, something indispensable for spiritual creativity.

6. *Examination of Prayer*

This last point of prayer is one of the most important and should be written out. It is the bridge to discernment. In fact, the examination of prayer is already an exercise of discernment, insofar as whoever prays must already make the choice of what to consider. It is here that the "stuff" of true and proper discernment is gathered. First, we try to preserve what God seems to be suggesting to us; afterward, we note thoughts of uncertain origin.

Examination of prayer is useful, because by means of it we see from moment to moment which thoughts the Holy Spirit speaks to our hearts and by means of which feelings God awakens his thoughts in us. We see even better where we are putting up resistance, where our attachments, our stubbornness, or our sensual pleasures lie. From examination, we are also able to glimpse possible deceptions, and therefore, from moment to moment and prayer to prayer, we ourselves can improve our attitudes and strategies of prayer.

The examination of prayer is important for growing in one's relationship with the Lord. Prayer can easily become rote, a habit, or degenerate from a true conversation with God to one in which one is actually only alone with one's own thoughts. If instead I am attentive to what is happening in each encounter, in each prayer period, I grow in wisdom because I have an open, constant dialogue in which rapport is built and grows in an organic, authentic, and living way. If I remember something from every encounter I have with others, it would truly be an absurd negligence not to develop a memory of my encounters with God. We see this memory of encounters in the Scriptures. Religion is, above all, a spiritual memory.

(For an example of a written examination, see p. 80).

How to Use Examinations of Prayer

At this point you need to work with the written pairs of thoughts and feelings noted in the review of prayer. Ask yourself if the thought will bind you closer to God, make you more like God, and deepen your commitment to God. If the answer is positive, write this thought on a new sheet of paper titled *thoughts inspired by the Holy Spirit*. Do the same with the feelings, noting on a fresh sheet of paper the *feelings inspired by the Holy Spirit*. If the thoughts and feelings do not help you to entrust yourself to God, but lead to resistance and a sense of being locked up in yourself, copy these thoughts or feelings onto still other sheets of paper, titled respectively *thoughts inspired by the enemy* and *feelings inspired by the enemy*. In the end each thought/ feeling pair that was written in the examination of prayer now has been transcribed onto separate sheets of paper.

❀ ❀

THOUGHTS	FEELINGS
A. At this moment God wants to tell me... and I write down the thoughts that I believe God has told me.	*...raising in me the following feelings...* and I write down the corresponding feelings. *Note:* It could also be the reverse: from a feeling, or state of being, thoughts are brought forth.
B. Also, at this moment the following thoughts come to mind... and I write some down, the most important, the most interesting.	*...these thoughts provoke in me the following feelings...* and I write them down on the line corresponding to the thought.
C. The following temptations and distractions also come to mind... and I write them down.	*...which cause the following feelings in me...* and I write them down.
Note: For each of these, it is best to write one, or at the most, two things.	

For greater clarity, let us take an example. Let's suppose I've written down this examination of prayer: "At this moment, God wanted to tell me that he is holy and faithful. This has kindled in me a feeling of unease, of fear." The thought evidently impels me toward God, and therefore I write it on the sheet where I gather the thoughts suggested by the Holy Spirit. The feeling does not help to thrust me toward God in the same direction as the thought, and therefore I move it to the sheet of feelings inspired by the enemy. It is clear that the holiness and faithfulness of God frighten me, perhaps because I perceive this as something that will make demands on me. I might have to renounce something I like or be faithful to something I do not like. Before drawing conclusions, however, it is important to reflect on what the other thoughts written down in the examination of the prayer indicate. Often they also have to do with what I have identified as the main spiritual fruit of this hour of prayer.

In the example given, if I continue to reflect I might gradually be able to glimpse the motivations of my fear. If I pay attention to the feeling of fear, from it will emerge the realization of why I have this fear or of what I am afraid.

Through this process of contemplative "analysis," the content of my prayer examinations are assigned to four separate sheets of paper: 1) The thoughts I recognize as raised by the Holy Spirit because they incline me toward God, toward my purification, toward a greater surrender to him; 2) the feelings recognized as raised by the Holy Spirit because they favor and sustain my steps of commitment to God and purifying penitence; 3) the thoughts recognized as inspired by the enemy because they advise me not to open myself to God too radically, instead to care for myself, to escape; 4) the feelings recognized as raised by the enemy, because they keep me occupied with myself, attentive to myself, and they nurture distrust of God or pessimism toward thoughts and feelings raised by the Holy Spirit.

Reflecting on the material written on these sheets I can begin to see with clarity how the Holy Spirit works in me, which thoughts to follow, which is my most spiri-

tual reasoning, which are the Holy Spirit's most perceptible points, which states of being to maintain and which
to avoid, which should not be welcomed or heeded,
which thoughts not to take seriously because they are
inspired by the tempter and if I were to follow them
would lead me to stray from the good path in life.

In listing together the thoughts that lead to God and
the feelings that favor surrender to God, I can see at a
glance the thoughts and feelings most helpful for spiritual
growth. Then I know what to pay attention to, what to
give weight to. I do the same thing with the thoughts and
feelings through which the tempter works. By doing this I
can achieve a significant level of spiritual self-knowledge. I
begin to notice patterns—the times, environments,
persons, relationships, reading, and tasks that are
conducive to a more spiritual attitude—and thus to my
salvation—and those that, instead, more easily subject me
to temptations or which should even be avoided because
they pose the real risk of sin. We need to highlight immediately that at this point, I am seeing only patterns. I
should be careful about drawing absolute conclusions at
this point, even if I reach these conclusions after opening
myself to the Lord in prayer. It is really true wisdom that I
need, a wisdom that is, at the same time, my very health.
This wisdom comes from discernment.

How to Begin the Process of Discernment

In order to begin the first stage of discernment it is
necessary to enter into a regular rhythm of prayer. A
person could make a retreat, dedicating several days
exclusively to spiritual exercises, or time for prolonged
prayer could be planned into the regular daily routine.

In this second case, the time reserved for prayer should be an hour at the minimum, using the prayer method presented above. In either case, the ideal would be to be accompanied by a guide who is steeped in the spiritual tradition of the Church. A guide for discernment should be immersed not only in the spiritual wisdom of the tradition, but also attentive to contemporary cultural and psycho-spiritual movements.

We begin the process of discernment with Sacred Scripture, with the fundamental themes of our faith, and with a good biblical commentary. Using a commentary should not get us lost in the complexities of exegesis or a particular philosophical approach. Rather, a good commentary will disclose the texts in such a way that the inner dynamics of the chosen verses might appear. In turn, this should allow us to place the texts within the great arc of the Bible, within the great, intelligible, and organic dynamic of revelation.[4]

Sacred Scripture, as the Word of God, is infused with the Holy Spirit, just as a piece of bread becomes soaked with wine when dipped in it. As I said before, when we listen to the Word and repeat it, the Holy Spirit acts in us and brings to light our shortcomings. Since this prayer proceeds—either in the form of an exhortation or the explanation of a biblical verse—through the exploration and confrontation of thoughts, a wide range of action is offered to the

Holy Spirit. Why? Let us suppose that I am fundamentally oriented toward myself. In this case, I recall that the Holy Spirit begins to act mainly by moving my rational dimension toward new, Gospel-oriented thoughts. By meditating on a profoundly moving thought from Sacred Scripture it is my reasoning faculty that is most directly addressed.

Thus, it is the reason, with its reflective activity, that is most open to the Holy Spirit's action, especially if we are fundamentally tied to our own shells, to our own wills, with sentimental attachments to our egos. But watch what happens if our minds begin to grasp the suggestion of the Word of God, which the Holy Spirit illuminates with brief, lucid flashes of clear realization that this is the path of true life. Anxiety and doubts immediately begin to arise as previously described. This is the point at which we can truly enter into the process of discernment. It is important therefore that we begin to notice the movements that warn us of resistance or acceptance of thoughts suggested in the method of prayer.

If, instead, one were already oriented toward Christ and no longer seeking to affirm one's own will but to follow the path of the Lord, then the Word of God is nothing less than one's favorite food. And since one's emotional dimension is still being nourished by truly spiritual consolation, thanks to the Word of God, the Holy Spirit acts on one's reason and strengthens one's spiritual awareness, supplying reasons, diminishing obstacles, and encouraging one in good. In no way does this cause violence to the person, for the Holy Spirit approaches each one precisely with what is best for that person.

It takes a few days praying with a Scripture passage in this manner to begin to feel the warmth that is characteristic of the consolation of the Holy Spirit. We are led in this way to the conclusive moment of purification, the moment of penitence and warmth in which we finally feel the gaze of the Lord's boundless mercy upon us. If we dedicate, every now and then, a more intense period of time to prayer, we will have discovered a helpful secret for maintaining spiritual health. It can happen that "professional" religious and those who take prayer and the spiritual life very seriously could fall into the trap of feeling they are advanced, already set, and have already learned what they need to know. When they meditate on a Bible passage as explained in the manner indicated above, they could think that there is nothing new, that they already know everything. Such an attitude reveals that deep down they risk returning to navel-gazing, to a life managed according to their own wills. If they were actually oriented toward the Lord in a crystal-clear way, they would react in the typical way of those who, fundamentally open to God's life, *rejoice* in the spiritual food they have found. Using a common yet eloquent example, we could think of a man in love with a woman. He often feels like telling his love that she is beautiful. He would not tell himself, "I'm not going to say it to her. It's already been heard before; this is nothing new." That would be ludicrous precisely because it is the strength of feeling that pushes him to express his love. But the strength of this feeling depends on the strength of the tie, of the love, of the attraction and the unity that he has with the woman.

Often, people who believe they are spiritually mature betray themselves in a kind of "snobbery" that reveals a type of jealousy, of envy, of competition, and a measuring themselves against someone who is teaching or sharing a spiritual text. The jealousy that impedes people from rejoicing that another speaks of God is the sin of those who are divorced from love, who no longer feel involved in love, and who thus no longer reason with the mind of love. If they truly loved God, they would rejoice that someone else also speaks well of, proclaims, and announces God.

The initial reaction this prayer based on the Word of God arouses in me begins to expose to me what I am actually seeking in life, what my heart holds most important and, therefore, what is my true orientation. It is much more difficult to come to these discoveries through sentimental sharing, which without prayer is about as effective as abstract, rationalistic preaching.

The Path to Forgiveness

Faithfully Following Spiritual Thoughts and Feelings

Sensing our first inner movements, we embark upon the path of discernment, aiming at real and personal encounters with God the Father. If we use this method of prayer, especially with the examination at the end, we will have in our hands the evidence of what is happening within us. It is helpful to remember that it is not so important to succeed in what we want to do. We shouldn't dramatize what is happening. But what is important is to do this exercise well and write down in a notebook the thoughts and significant feelings that come to us. This is how we enrich the "material" that will be revealed to us as how the spirit of God is acting in us, and how we are being tempted.

Let us do all this to follow the thoughts and feelings through which the Holy Spirit works, and to disregard the thoughts and feelings that subject us to temptation and, therefore, through which the tempter works more easily. Discernment thus leads us to acquire and maintain an attitude of docility, which is a dimension of authentic humility. It is necessary to accept the spiritual struggle and to maintain that contemplative attitude characterized by letting go of protagonism in prayer, and instead being capable of welcoming and thus of patience.

It may happen that, after the first spiritual movements, prayer seems to be immensely difficult. Above all, it may be difficult even to begin. One hour may seem extremely long. While we are praying, the end may seem nowhere in sight, and we might be tempted to shorten the time or not to begin at all, putting prayer off until later. Or else the path might seem too demanding. We might think of all the other people in the Church and in the world who do not take prayer seriously, and who nonetheless are just fine. We then ask ourselves: "Why do I have to take things so seriously?"

We might begin to think that the spiritual life is too complicated and demanding, that we can get by with less, and that, after all, we already know enough about it and don't want anything more. Furthermore, we might think that now we only have to live what we have already understood and felt. At such times, only an authentically contemplative attitude, patient and obedient, can help us recover the correct attitude. In this situation, we need to do more than try. It is essential to react firmly against this state of mind.

If I react against these thoughts and decide to lengthen my prayer a bit or not to do something else that is pleasurable for my senses, then I need to make this decision while dialoguing with God in prayer. It is not necessary for me to react against these states of lethargy relying solely on the strength of my own will or the steadfastness of my own decisions, because this is precisely what the enemy is expecting. In fact, this is how I put myself on the slippery slope of affirming my own will, contrary to salvation. The true medicine for this spiritual situation is to react by holding more firmly to my relationship with the Lord.

Stop Not, Except Before the Crucified Lord

It is necessary to take into account that I will probably go through moments of difficulty, of spiritual dryness, of discouragement, of the pain of discovering mistakes, the real errors and sins of my past life. It is not very pleasant coming to understand that deep down I have sought to do my own will, that I have justified with elegance, with reasons often disguised by religious motivations, a life in which I was in charge. I have to be attentive at the moment of discouragement, when I begin to perceive sin as a reality of my life, that I don't fall into the trap of immediately seeking consolation from another person. Rather, I must remain on my path, knowing that the true Consoler is the Paraclete, the Holy Spirit.

Precisely because I have tried to assume a contemplative attitude in which I am not the protagonist, precisely because I seek to collaborate with the Holy

Spirit's action, or at least not be an obstacle to it, I become conscious of my sins and begin to see them in a spiritual key, that is, as a stimulus for seeking the Lord. The realization that I am a sinner increases the unhappiness in my heart, the sorrow; perhaps it can also give rise to a certain self-deprecation and dejection, but at the same time I intuit that my sins propel me forward in my urgency to see the Savior's Face. The encounter with this Face is not an easy solution to the anguish I feel for my sins, but it is a gesture of love in which God compromises himself. I become sad and weep for Christ in his passion, and my sins begin to join with his wounds more and more, not as the perception of guilt but as a healing and the incomprehensible folly of his love, which not only heals my sins but enflames my love with this love for my Savior who for me allowed himself to be inflicted with pain. Thus, in a real way, I experience Jesus' taking my pains upon himself, being pierced for my crimes, so that by his bruises I am healed (cf. Is 53:4–5).

> The realization that I am a sinner increases the unhappiness in my heart...but at the same time I intuit that my sins propel me forward in my urgency to see the Savior's Face.

The true spiritual movement leads us toward Calvary to find the Crucified One in our own hands, handed over to us sinners that he might touch us with love. We have a false fear of God. Our distrust of him makes us unable to hand our lives over to him. But God himself takes the first step. He loves us first and offers himself to us to make us see that he believes us worthy of *his* confidence. Only when the flesh of the old self dies in the death of Christ are we able to make gestures of trust in the Lord. And there on Calvary we experience salvation.

Especially today when the psyches of the younger generations are so fragile and incapable of confronting solitude, psychological pressures could press one to confess one's sins without real contrition. That is, as soon as one commits a sin, one immediately runs to confess it, thinking that in this way one has already achieved purification. It is helpful to recall the tradition of the ancient Church that had a specific time for the penitent to prepare for Reconciliation.

The person must not become the victim of his or her own psychological pressures, but the psyche, with all its anguish and urgency, should open itself to the spiritual dynamic in such a way that the sacrament of Reconciliation is not seen primarily as a psychological release, but as an act of faith from which even the psyche can draw well-being. For this to happen, as we have already seen, we must allow ourselves to be led by our thoughts to the realization within us of the sin, that is, to admit we are sinners because, in one way or another, we have often chosen to make ourselves the center of everything, whether through our thoughts and rationalizations, or through our feelings and a sensual life, or through the trivial imposition of our own wills, and so on.

My self-love becomes apparent in a subtle way when I admit my sin and then assign to myself a penance. I say to myself: "Yes, I get it. I've sinned. I did this and that, but it was because I didn't know who God truly was and how God saved me. But now I know. Now I understand.

From now on I won't do that anymore. Instead, Lord, I'm sorry, and I promise I'll do this and that other penance, this and that other sacrifice, because I've sinned. From now on, Lord, you can bet that I'll do this and I'll be careful about that," and so on.

The problem with this reasoning is that it is completely locked up in the "I." I seem to be talking with God, but I am really speaking to myself. The reasoning never breaks through into true relationship, never goes out of itself, but continues to act according to my own will, proposing sacrifices, improvements, missions, heroic acts, pious works—all suggested by me.

Instead, those who follow the proper spiritual movement no longer see their sin with their own eyes. They realize how futile this is, since after so many years of trying it nothing has happened. Now they begin to see their sin as Christ sees it, as he takes it on himself. They begin to see how Christ has saved them. They understand better and ascertain ever more clearly that they no longer have anything to offer because they cannot keep and carry out their promises. Everything is an absolutely free and unmerited gift.

They recognize themselves more and more in the image of Peter in the courtyard of the high priest. Peter, having spent all his promises and oaths before a servant girl, is completely naked, unarmed, and annihilated in his pride. He, a person who wants to *merit* mercy and forgiveness, is struck by a gaze of unexpected goodness and mercy. Unless we truly pray—not in some way feign prayer or simply carry on a monologue—then the sins that begin to emerge in our lives could knock us down so that we not only fall into lethargy—a sort of spiritual laziness—but immediately we feel ourselves irrevocably separated from God. And if God seems too far away, we can begin to suffer a false spiritual "inferiority complex," believing it impossible that God could forgive us or save us, or that we could ever change our lives. This is the reaction of the heart of one who has fallen into temptation, to the point that one doesn't even believe that God could change one's life or give one the strength to change. This heart remains anchored in itself, in its own strengths, where there actually is no hope. This person distrusts God precisely because there is no movement toward trust in him.

In this state, hope and charity, just as faith itself, are not attainable realities. If I reason only within my own ego, then hope becomes either an illusion or a utopia that, once disappointed, brings me down even further. Charity grows weary of always having to love or else it is perverted into self-love. Self-love declares that it is impossible to live the faith and the Gospel without destroying oneself. The Gospel demands bitter sacrifices, which is fine for heroes who can boast of having fulfilled them, but I am not one of them.

Through Spiritual Desolation

Those who attend to inner spiritual movements with serene openness walk with great balance through desolation and consolation. This is because, fundamentally, these people do not take desolation or consolation too seriously, realizing they are only indications, signs, means, and that the *goal* is an encounter with the Lord. The most important thing is perseverance. We must persevere along the road we have undertaken until reaching our goal, above all when it is difficult and we are caught up in desolation. Without perseverance, when discouraged because of our own weaknesses and sins or when faced with the evil of the world, we will be tempted to stop, to be content with where we are in the spiritual life, or to cut back on our prayer. Persons who have a true contemplative attitude persevere, knowing that thoughts that arise at the moment of dejection, desolation, or discouragement are not inspired by the Holy Spirit and should not be followed. Attentiveness, therefore, to desolation and to moments of emptiness and dryness, is important. Speaking about these experiences with a spiritual person is valuable, since they can also be moments of sustenance from God, and the help of a spiritual guide can protect us from deceptions.

Desolation can appear in another form. There are people who have a great need to be affirmed and easily attribute small spiritual results to their own merits. They think that, since they have always been good at everything, they must be doing well even in this, and even more the results they see in their spiritual lives must be a result of their efforts. The risk is real that we could lock ourselves up in our egos and base our spiritual lives on feelings. It is then that the Lord can leave us in solitude, in emptiness, so that we realize that it is God's grace that enflames our hearts and that only through the gift of love can we reach the taste of love. We cannot imagine love. For one who is easily led to enthusiasm and euphoria, the Lord might take away strong feelings and the psychological effects of prayer so that one might more objectively discover one's personal reality and see what one is truly capable of. The Lord does not want such a person to waste time with great promises and projects since, if the person is not sufficiently satisfied, he or she will pull the oars back into the boat.

Opening Oneself to Spiritual Relationships

The spiritual masters unanimously insist that we must not dialogue with temptation. As soon as I begin to have a certain clarity about which thoughts orient me toward the Lord and which feelings warm me toward him, I must hold firm to that orientation. Thoughts or feelings that present themselves with vehemence and urgency, disturbing and frightening me, are better told to a truly spiritual person who knows how to defuse temptations. (One should never speak of one's temptations with those who are not experts in the spiritual struggle. Such persons could themselves fall into the trap of the same temptation or cause the person who confided the temptation to get caught up in it because they do not consider it from a spiritual perspective.)

Above all, it is helpful to reveal temptations that we feel we should keep to ourselves because they seem too personal or private, something that should remain a secret. Temptation revealed to a spiritual person disappears like ice in an oven. Exposing the enemy's temptations is true preventative medicine. What actually happens in such a spiritual conversation? In opening ourselves to a spiritual relationship, we open ourselves to the Lord. In the beginning there is the risk that, in our minds, the Lord is an abstract, conceptual reality or a psychological need, but precisely through this ecclesial or directly liturgical approach of spiritual guidance we are able to open ourselves to the Lord's otherness. It is communion with God that conquers evil, dissipates darkness, and gives life to our hearts.

The Founding Experience of God-Love

The first stage of discernment comes to an end when, suffocating in the darkness of the night, we smell death, as Lazarus did, feeling ourselves to be wrapped in a shroud and left in the tomb. Like Lazarus, however, we too hear the voice that calls us out of the grave. For sinners, this is a new creation in which we come back to a regenerated life. From now on we will always see life in a different light. It is no longer an uncontrollable tragic course toward a sealed tomb, but it gushes forth from a tomb that is open.

In the *Spiritual Exercises*, Ignatius of Loyola concluded the first phase of the spiritual journey in hell, where the person observes in an existential, rational-experiential way the absurdity and nothingness of a life without God. If we separate life and God, we live an illusion. Ignatius begins the journey of the second phase with the Lord's call, because in the spiritual person, vocation, creation, and redemption coincide.

The first stage of discernment comes to an end when we allow ourselves to be reached by Christ, welcomed by him, caught up in his embrace. We allow the Lord to throw his arms around us while we, with all our wounds and exposed to temptations, finally murmur with our whole being: "Jesus Christ, my Lord and my Savior, make me according to your holy will." Reached by love in the splendor of the new creation, we can now carry out the supreme act of love and faith: offering our own wills to the will of the Lord who not only wants the good, but who also truly possesses it and therefore can realize it.

This act of faith and love is indispensable if we want to begin to create, to construct, and to fulfill ourselves. It is only by sharing the experience of St. Peter, weeping in the high priest's courtyard after encountering the eyes of merciful Love, that we can understand that it is through self-renunciation that we find ourselves anew. It is through the death of our own wills that our true wills made in the image of agape no longer die. In this act of faith, God's love touches the human heart in a perceptible way so that even the flesh is aware of being redeemed.

Just as the woman in the Gospel of Mark (5:24–34) felt in her body that she had been healed, we sense that in the strength of Christ's flesh exposed to the evil of the world we find our flesh in his wounds and can recognize him as our Lord. It is truly an act of faith in which we, caught up in God's ecstasy, go out of ourselves and, in the wake of divine love, return to God, affirming him as the Lord, the One, the Incomparable.

Now we cannot make this act of faith and love on our own. For each of us, this work is only possible in the Holy Spirit, who makes God, "*my* God," and salvation, "*my* salvation." We experience this theological reality precisely because we have allowed ourselves to be guided by the Holy Spirit and, through discernment, have become more fully and radically disposed to his presence and action. For this reason, at the moment when we fall into the Lord's arms, we leave behind the dimension of slavery and finally say, "Abba, Father." Then Christ, to whom we have entrusted ourselves, becomes the sphere in which we discover that we are sons and daughters of God.

This whole process is not a "mystical" episode or some psychological conviction, but an event that happens in the light of the sun, in the Church, and in a liturgy, that is, in the sacrament of Reconciliation. The sacrament of forgiveness is a liturgy and therefore a language that is addressed to the whole person and also makes the whole person speak. For this reason it is an encounter, an event, in which we perceptibly receive the eternal realities. Reconciliation and forgiveness do not bring about chiefly psychological effects since, because of our histories, our characters, and other reasons, we often do not *feel* forgiven—perhaps even for a long time. However, because of the trust we have experienced, we will believe ourselves to be forgiven sinners, and slowly this forgiveness will permeate our entire beings.

Reconciliation is a liturgy that, as such, expres-ses the entire truth of Christ in all its objectivity. A real and true encounter occurs between two personal objectivities: that of the sinner and that of the Savior. Forgiveness doesn't mean simply that God has cancelled our sins, but that God takes upon himself the life we lived without him. What has been emptied by our selfishness, the devastating power that deprives life of its true meaning, is now filled by grace and illuminated by true meaning.

> Forgiveness doesn't mean simply that God has cancelled our sins, but that God takes upon himself the life we lived without him.

In forgiveness, a Christian rediscovers his or her complete life, gathered in Christ's merciful gaze. All of one's personal history becomes a spiritual reality because of the organic sense of all of life in Christ. Therefore, even what was sin now calls God to mind, speaks of him, and holds the forgiven sinner tightly to his or her Creator and Savior. The penance given will be a type of *pharmakos*, a *paideia*, a salutary, pedagogical path to developing a living memory of forgiveness. The most important reality is that forgiveness is not limited to the person to whom it has been given, but expands to the whole Church. To discover ourselves as sons and daughters of God means to discover our brothers and sisters, or at least to begin walking on the path to discovering the faces of our brothers and sisters.

Guarding the Desire for Forgiveness

Forgiveness is the foundational event in every Christian's life. The Christian journey, in fact, begins with Baptism, which, as Origen says, is a general and gratuitous pardon. However, as Truhlar recalls, Baptism, administered to children who are then submersed in a culture which is not that of Baptism, often remains buried. Reconciliation is thus the moment in which all the splendor, force, and efficacy of Baptism return to the light. That is why, for many Christians, the truly foundational beginning of their lives was Reconciliation, when they were consciously able to relive forgiveness.

Only God can forgive sins. Therefore no other reality can present itself to us with the certainty of being an experience of God as can forgiveness. We often find people who speak of their disappointment because certain retreats and prayers, which they had considered authentic experiences of God, after a time came to be seen as self-inspired, as a type of psychotherapy. This is why the first stage of discernment ends with making the rationally reflected path coincide with the emotionally grasped realities, involving the whole human person. That is why the event has its own flavor, its own taste, which the person can gather rationally, memorize, and safeguard in the deposit of the sentiment's experience, while the will is decidedly oriented to the foundational event itself.

The principal themes of faith—creation, sin, redemption, the Church, and the Trinity—thus become, in the mind of the forgiven sinner, the path through which memory, taste, and creativity find again the unity once destroyed by sin. A Christian who has followed the paths of prayer and discernment begins to think within the framework of salvation history. The horizon of thought becomes lived theology, and it is impossible to be satisfied with teachers who propose only the world's thought.

The exercise of memory is important. From now on the spiritual life can be healthy only if it is given constant care. A large part of spiritual life will be safeguarding the purified heart, the taste for the Word of God, the delight of forgiveness, and the taste for the Holy Spirit's action. I speak of desire and not just of sentiment. Desire is a reality indicating a greater integration than just sentiment. In order to identify a desire, the participation of the entire person is necessary. The healed human heart knows its desire, recognizes the flavors that give it life.

One of the paths to take in safeguarding the flavor and desire of God is certainly the memory of the event of forgiveness itself. And what is the most authentic memory of forgiveness? To repeat and relive the prayer we made when asking with our whole being for forgiveness. When we ask for forgiveness, we are already caught up by God's love. Asking for forgiveness means entering into the state of repentance. When we become aware of sin, we overcome the psychology of guilt, imperfections, and errors, and we enter into the dimension of faith. One can only understand sin within faith, and the one who knows oneself to be a sinner now sees the Lord knocking with mercy at the heart's threshold.

Without faith we perceive ourselves unequal to the task of the spiritual life. We believe we are not as we should be or would like to be, imperfect and not in conformity with the law. In faith we can feel ourselves to be sinners because we know that sin has to do with relationship, with love, with the face of the other, the Face of God. The repentance that flows forth from deep within us is a cry, a sob, a pain, as if our hearts were broken in a million pieces. It is a pain that once held our hearts tightly in its fist because we felt we had to save ourselves; then our tears were tears of sadness. And in that state the pain became unbearable. We gave in and welcomed the Lord who threw his arms around us. Everything we believed important fell to pieces; then this pain was transformed into birthing pains, and the tears were transformed into tears of joy, of celebration.

It is not the heart that was shattered, but rather the shell in which the heart was locked. Now our hearts can beat freely. Repentance is a movement that urges us toward God's embrace. It is like a child when her mother tells her something she does not like. The child plays the victim, wants to leave her mother, draws away, but then immediately is sorry. Silently she goes back into the room, a small sob is heard, a rushing toward her mother, whispering whatever words. Repentance is a movement that inserts us into the wave of gratuitous relationships, where even a fault is understood in terms of a more genuine, closer relationship, and therefore in terms of God's Face.

When instead we approach Reconciliation without repentance, asking for forgiveness more from psychological pressure than a contrite heart, we do not sense God's Face but our own inadequacy, the rule, the law, the commandment that cannot satisfy. It is confession more for the sake of ourselves than passionate love for a God who has touched us. Repentance is the measure of the authenticity of the path we have taken. For this reason the most secure memory of forgiveness, of the taste of love, is the prayer that safeguards the memory of forgiveness. It is a type of *penthos*, keeping alive in our hearts the effect of repentance. It is the rediscovery of love. I repeat the words I used when I asked for forgiveness, but I cry sweet tears, the tears of the celebration that has overwhelmed me with rediscovered love.

The best memory, therefore, is focusing attention on the first touch of love on the penitent heart. This means constantly maintaining a living awareness of the effect of repentance, of forgiveness, and of rediscovered love. The philokalic Fathers would call such a memory "temperance." Temperance is paying attention to the realities that remain, that carry weight, that is, paying attention to the reality of God. Our attention is steadiest when it is focused on a desire. Where the attention lies, there lies the person's intellect—the intellect in a spiritual sense. When the attention is on the memory of the love experienced, the intellect, recalled to this reality of love, also discovers there its authentic place, that is, its true foundation.

It is at this point that the person achieves the highest personal integration or wholeness. Such a person becomes creative in a crystalline, pure sense, without ambiguous interests or self-seeking, but with a true, proper, and gratuitous impulse. This creativity is enveloped by the realities that remain, because they set out from and flow back to love: "Remain in my love."

A Warning

As said before, spiritual masters insist discernment should take place in a spiritual dialogue. From what we've covered up to this point, it's clear that there is no simple path in discerning. In fact, there are many traps along the way. Therefore, it's worth repeating the ancient counsel of seeking a companion on this path.

Moreover, although discernment is the art that saves us from exaggerations and deviations and guarantees wisdom, it is not the path for everyone. It is possible to live a Christian life, as we well know, limiting ourselves to treading the path others have taken before us on the journey of faith, repeating their gestures, habits, customs, and slowly discovering the conscious and personal dimension of salvation.

The fact remains, however, that the cultural changes our age is subjected to make such a life extremely difficult, because these cultural differences divide even members of the same family. The art of discernment, it seems, perfectly responds to the situation today in which the social, cultural, and ecclesial fabric is pulled apart by so many changes and is in an age of transition. The Church herself, through her documents, continually invites us to an exercise of discernment. The very tradition of the Church testifies to the fact that discernment is the royal way for the believer, an art of synergy with God's gift, a guide to listening to the tradition, an ecclesial incardination, an openness to history, and a psycho-spiritual exercise.

> The art of discernment... perfectly responds to the situation today in which the social, cultural, and ecclesial fabric is pulled apart by so many changes and is in an age of transition.

Clearly, for the person who has reached a strong and personal identification of the desire and taste of salvation, life will be very different than for the one who moves within the general framework of precepts and rules, that is, in the cultural, moral, and psychological vortex of our times. Whoever has arrived at a memory of God already begins the day differently, because that person begins to recognize within the world's perfumes, flavors, and tastes what is of God and what is not. Such a person confronts with a different attitude the dawning day, with its activities and encounters, and therefore also ends the day differently, gathering its fruits.

In the swirl of flavors and fragrances offered by the world, which often leaves people today uneasy, it is very difficult to profess doctrines and precepts without having an inner conviction that fills the heart and gives its own flavor. Those who, instead, discover with certainty God's action within them and are able to identify it, are preserved from dogmatism, fundamentalism, laxity, and psychologism. They enter the second stage of discernment, where they work on discerning between different possibilities of good until their desire for God, through many exercises in discernment, consolidates into a constant attitude of discernment.

Communal discernment is frequently spoken of today. After exploring the principal characteristics of this first stage of discernment, however, caution is advised regarding communitarian discernment. If members of the community are strongly attached to their own wills and seek to run their own lives and that of the community or institute according to their own visions—even if they do so using the most "spiritual" motivations—then it is clear that communal discernment will not be possible. Those who have already acquired a knowledge of God and who reason with a spiritual mentality will read realities such as the cross, difficulties, illnesses, the resistance and failures of others differently than those with a non-spiritual mentality. Some would see in events their exquisitely salvific and spiritual meaning, while others would still be fighting to carry out their own visions. The former would have not only the art but also the attitude of discernment, and thus would grasp life's events in sapiential terms, finding in them their spiritual meaning. The latter would fight with difficulties and welcome only what is fulfilled according to their ideas.

It is difficult to carry out a communal discernment process. Communities often make the effort at least to reach a level of fraternal sharing, conversation, an exchange of views, but it needs to be said that this is not a true and proper discernment. Properly speaking, for communal discernment to take place, it is necessary that all the members of the community have completed the first stage of discernment and reached a fundamental spiritual understanding. The effort that many are making to reach this point must be appreciated, especially since the post-conciliar Church shows us that wherever there is a community of two, three, or more persons who are truly in agreement with the Lord, there life flowers.

PART II
How to Remain with Christ

CHAPTER 4

The Principle and Foundation of Discerning How to Remain in Christ

Finding Ourselves in Christ[1]

DISCERNMENT IN THE SECOND STAGE,[2] that of the *sequela Christi*, has its principle and foundation in the experience into which we have been led by the first stage. We have seen how the movements of the first stage of discernment lead a believer to a rational-experiential knowledge of self-in-God and of God in his or her history. It deals with a knowledge of self in one's own truth, growing in the capacity to see oneself as God does. At the same time, however, this stage purifies one's idea of God, slowly dismantling the false images one has of God, bringing one to a realistic and true awareness, and finally discovering God as the founding and absolute "Thou" not only of one's life, but also of the entire history of the universe. All this happens in an experience of God as one's merciful Father revealed in creation and redemption as Love.

The Holy Spirit makes this revelation personal for every sincere person who seeks God. Through his action we experience God as our Father, and the Son—in whom we were created and saved—as our Lord and Savior. The Holy Spirit attracts us with a love that brings us to establish personal relationships with God. One of the greatest qualifying moments of such a relationship is the experience of forgiveness. It is precisely in forgiveness that we come to the certainty of the experience of God and, therefore, of the salvation that is truly ours. Only God forgives sins. Only God can bring the dead back to life, making we who are sinners—slaves of ourselves and of the self-asserting and self-destructive forces within us—into sons and daughters capable of relating gratuitously with ourselves as well as others and the world, because we know ourselves to be madly loved by the Father.

The one who is dead, as Lazarus in the tomb, hears the voice that calls him or her forth (cf. Jn 11:43). At that moment, instead of a stone sealing the tomb the person finds the Father throwing his arms around him or her. In this event one experiences not only the forgiveness of individual sins, but the Father's forgiveness of all one's sins. One has been washed clean. All at once one sees that one's sins have been in some way a choice, and that perhaps one's openness to God was only a pretense.

At this moment our eyes are completely opened. This is an experience of being healed, a taste of the new creation that imprints itself on our hearts and our senses, but also on our feelings and our reason. It is a precise flavor, an unmistakable taste. It is a foundational event for all of our faculties. For some, this moment coincides with Baptism. For others—already baptized, but with their Baptism "buried" in selfishness and closed within themselves—it is a radical reconciliation. In any case, it deals with a new creation, because it leads us back to living the radical newness constituted by Baptism, its general and gratuitous pardon.

Reconciliation is the work of the Holy Spirit, because it is in the Holy Spirit that sins are forgiven. Only the Holy Spirit communicates God and God's love in this personal way and disposes us to welcome God, moving the human heart toward a mature love that freely surrenders itself into the hands of the Lord who comes. Only the Holy Spirit can lift us to the intelligence of a mature love ready to renounce the selfish principle of self-assertion and self-salvation—the only way to be saved. But we can do this only because God

> Only the Holy Spirit can lift us to the intelligence of a mature love ready to renounce the selfish principle of self-assertion and self-salvation.

himself first lives in ecstasy and *kenosis*, an ecstasy that for God is *kenosis*, the abandonment of his absoluteness and the descent to creation.

The whole Trinity is involved in this process of *kenosis*. It is the Trinity who sends humanity the Second Person, the Word of God, the Son in whose image humanity was created. The Holy Spirit makes the Word flesh, who is born of the Virgin as a Child, as a Son, and who grows among us, taking upon himself all the dimensions of history and human life, especially those of sin and death. At the event of the passion, Jesus entrusts himself entirely into our hands and he lives humanity's filial surrender to God the Father.

The relationship we have with God is thus founded and fulfilled in the coming of the Son of God, in his incarnation, passion, and return to the Father. Our relationship with God is possible because God first related to us (cf. 1 Jn 4:10). God the Father established in Christ a relationship with humanity. Christ is also humanity's one and complete possibility of relationship with God. Our faith is always a response to the love with which God has joined us to himself.

We can believe in God and relate to God because God has established a relationship with us and has opened the way for us to return to him. Christ, God's ecstasy toward humanity, is also our ecstasy toward God. The Holy Spirit guides every believer in this relationship with God, so that Christ becomes Lord for each of us. In the Holy Spirit each of our paths in Christ is a completely personal one, even if we walk together with others who have been baptized.

Christ, true God and true man, is the divine Person who contains within himself the experience of the love of God and of humanity. In the foundational experience of faith—that is, in the real encounter with Christ who forgives our sins and saves us—we savor God's love, we taste a personal love. Christ does not communicate to us something abstract but a reality we are meant to experience, to taste, to live. For this reason the salvation Christ communicates with his forgiveness is a salvation that has the characteristics of Christ, *his* flavor, *his* truth, that we nevertheless experience as our own. In radical forgiveness, in true reconciliation, we recognize ourselves in Christ.

We feel ourselves a part of his love, of his reality. We perceive that Christ belongs to us and that everything that belongs to Christ is also ours. It's like the experience of reading a piece of poetry and crying out: "This is exactly what *I* wanted to say, but I didn't know how to express it!"

In the experience of forgiveness, Christians surrender to Christ because they discover themselves *in* Christ, as if they are what Christ is, as if they are what Christ experiences in his divine-human love, as if they were now all they would have desired to be at the end of creation. All at once, Baptism, in which their surrender has its foundation, becomes real, living. The heart of the Christian, with all its cognitive and sensitive capacities, begins to savor Christ who is the love that unites God and humanity.

The Memory of Salvation in Christ— The Beginning of Discernment[3]

After having experienced forgiveness, a real encounter with God, I surrender to the Lord, seeking to make this foundational event a lasting memory. It is a memory of love that permeates all my faculties, which are rooted in and grafted on love: my reason, sentiment, will, intuition, etc., and even my sensory perception. This memory, this safeguarded taste, becomes the authentic starting point of discernment. When I eat, my sense of taste, if it is healthy, is capable of distinguishing good food from bad. In the same way, the spiritual taste preserved in my memory can identify what is connatural with it from what is not.

Many ancient spiritual writers spoke of how to maintain this constant memory of what God has worked in us, and they suggested, for example, the exercise of temperance. Temperance is the spiritual attitude of those who have their attention focused on what counts, on what remains, on what truly carries weight. This attention focuses all their faculties in Christ and protects them from the excitement and disturbance of their passions.

Now, from the moment one encounters God in an authentic and true forgiveness, where the Lord not only forgives sin but saves the sinner, temperance keeps one's attention focused on the salvific love one has experienced. It is a love that has a Face—Christ—but also a concrete flavor, a precise light. In order to be conserved this love needs progressively to permeate the entire person.

Furthermore, since our cognitive capacities are rooted in love and grow through love, temperance brings us to surrender our entire beings to love and thus brings about our real integration, a progressive unity, in which the different dimensions of our persons and the various facts of our lives are no longer lived as separate pieces that cause us unbearable suffering and confusion. We increasingly experience a more or less constant peace, that serenity that opens the intelligence to a certain creativity, so that we reach the goal of self-discovery and understand ourselves as children in the Son.

Only after experiencing something as foundational and all-embracing as a concrete and living memory of the taste of love can one interiorly unify oneself in a single, life-embracing orientation. Until this happens, one's search to overcome interior fractures and divisions often remains an exercise of the will, a moral imperative. We know, however, the usual outcome of such an approach.

Those whose intelligence has still in good part not been absorbed by the experience of a love that is real and true are easily distracted by attraction and flattery. Their lives are dispersed and shattered, as can be seen from the everyday micro-decisions they make to their major life choices. They are like those who are famished and grab any food they are offered. Or again, like someone who is curious and wants to listen to every voice, to capture every image.

Instead, temperate persons, whose intelligence and heart's attention are attracted by the Son's Face, do not feel the need to lose themselves in other things, to seek other "foods," which might be disgusting precisely because they have savored excellent, exquisite foods with unique flavors. It may seem that such persons have renounced many things, but their attitude is not dictated by a dry, imposed asceticism. Rather it is the consequence of a simple fidelity to the best, fidelity to something they have already tasted.

The attention of these persons is within their own hearts, where their spiritual intelligence expands into spiritual senses. They are therefore temperate and no longer feel an attraction for second- and third-rate things. Also, when the memory of this taste of God is difficult and they experience dryness, an exercise of patience is sufficient for them: remaining fully conscious that what they have tasted belongs to them and that nothing can cancel the foundational event that has regenerated their sensibility, senses, and thought. Even when salvation seems very distant, when the soul can't taste the memory and the mind struggles to concentrate, the asceticism the Christian has undertaken has its foundation in an encounter that has really taken place and is therefore rooted in a concrete love capable of bending the will in a healthy and correct way.

The conviction that one has tapped into true life, into an awareness of him who saves, and has been kissed by the Face of Love, safeguards the integrity of one's path and puts into perspective and unmasks temptations and the pressure of many attractions. Instead, those without such a foundational experience need immense willpower to concentrate on the Lord. Willpower, however, does not guarantee a true and conscious relationship with the Lord and the certainty of encountering him, since relying on willpower can often leave one feeling very alone as if cut off from the source of lifeblood. Those who impose such inflexibility on their lives easily swing like a pendulum from very rigid and ascetic behavior to behavior that is very libertine. Those with a foundational experience of love, on the other hand, experience asceticism as an art of guardianship rather than renunciation. They deny themselves on the strength of the precious gift, of the treasure that they have been given. This gives us a completely different view of Christian asceticism.

Asceticism is what the Holy Spirit encourages us to live as a *response* to our encounter with Christ, but it is not a way to reach him. We do not arrive at belief in Christ because we have made this choice and forced

> Asceticism is what the Holy Spirit encourages us to live as a *response* to our encounter with Christ, but it is not a way to reach him.

ourselves to carry it through. *We* are not the starting point of faith. Authentic Christian asceticism is based on gratitude for having been cleansed of one's sins (cf. 2 Pt 1:9). It directs every effort toward a life always more united with the Lord.

The Fundamental Rule of Discernment in Following Christ[4]

If we remember the movements of the Holy Spirit and the enemy spirit as described in the first stage of discernment, we can recall here the fundamental dynamic of how the Holy Spirit acts on persons who have radically chosen God, who let themselves be reached by God, and who have entered into relationship with God. All who are radically oriented toward God are offered spiritual consolation by the Holy Spirit, who works, above all, on the dimension of sentiment and desire. Even more, from the moment the intellects of these persons are nourished by spiritual tastes, the Holy Spirit also acts in the world of their thoughts, seeking to give reasons for this orientation to God and their surrender to him. Their thoughts then seek everything that has to do with God and the fulfillment of God's will. Since their thoughts then belong to God and they have handed themselves over to God, the Lord acts on them by acting *in* them. God enters into their hearts through their thoughts and feelings in a tender, kind way, seamlessly, without their feeling any force, any actions that are foreign to them, that might disturb, disquiet, sadden, or prick their consciences.

The thoughts and feelings inspired by the Holy Spirit present themselves in our hearts as an owner entering his own house, not knocking, not forcing open the door, but simply opening and entering because the house belongs to him. As a drop of water falls on a sponge and is silently absorbed without bouncing off or making noise, so the thoughts and feelings inspired by the Holy Spirit present themselves to the human heart. Or rather, they spring from the heart as an underground river simply appears. The heart recognizes these movements as its own, as belonging to it.

The enemy of human nature,[5] on the other hand, acts in a way contrary to the Holy Spirit. He acts above all on our thoughts, since the sentiment is occupied with our sensing and tasting love. The tempter pries into reason with violence, seeking to detach our thoughts from this orientation, to make us trip up. He presents obstacles, exaggerates struggles, renunciations, and sufferings. He multiplies the reasons for not going forward.... The enemy acts through disturbance, making the mind restless and provoking a certain state of fear, worry, and bewilderment. The enemy presents the journey as something strenuous and out of nowhere brings to mind dangers we had never imagined before.

The Deception of the Enemy Disguised as an Angel of Light[6]

The violent and disturbing ways of the enemy make it easy for the spiritual person to recognize temptation. While before our conversion both the enemy and the Holy Spirit can work in us by causing restlessness, after we have oriented our life entirely on Christ it is the enemy alone who disturbs and torments us. Therefore, at this point the thoughts that disturb, bite, disquiet, and sadden a person surrendered to the Lord are obviously inspired by the enemy. But if this were the entire story, the enemy would no longer be able to conquer spiritual persons because they would immediately recognize him by the fact that he inspires disturbing and disquieting thoughts. The enemy would be immediately recognized, like a thief who tries to break into a house. Given that the enemy cannot win because he would be immediately recognized, he disguises himself. From the angel of darkness the enemy turns into an angel of light (cf. 2 Cor 11:14) in order to tempt the spiritual person. This is the cardinal rule of all discernment in the second stage.

Whoever is in union with God cannot be tempted by obvious evil. The tempter realizes that such a person will reject the thoughts and states of being that are not from the Son or that are contrary to living as a child in the Son. He therefore presents himself through thoughts and states of being that *appear* spiritual so as to sneak into the spiritual person's world and then slowly break off his or her relationship with God the Father, reorient the person toward self, and enslave the person once more in his or her own little, self-managed world. The enemy, knowing that a spiritual person will not be suspicious of thoughts that urge him or her toward Christ and nourish the person's life with him, begins suggesting these spiritual thoughts to the soul.

The following is a simple example to help describe what I am talking about. Imagine a young man engaged to be married who goes to knock at the window of his fiancée one night. He calls her, she opens the window, and they speak. If another young man wanted her to open the window and tried to make her do so by banging on the window or shouting or trying to convince her with propositions of love, the young woman would immediately know that this was not her fiancé and would lock the window and close the curtains. If he were sly, however, this young man would watch the woman's fiancé and imitate his actions. He would knock as her lover does, imitating the sound of his voice, even saying the very same words. Then the woman might be fooled and open the window.

This is exactly the way the enemy operates with persons in the second stage of discernment. In entering into our souls the enemy tries to fool us, using thoughts and feelings similar to those inspired by the Holy Spirit. Spiritual persons use the art of discernment to discover the enemy's deceptions in order to grow in their spiritual lives in more complete conformity to Christ in their thinking, feeling, willing, and acting.

Chapter 5

Temptations

THE TEMPTATIONS THAT ARISE in following Christ at this stage, some of which we will now deal with, are very different from the temptations we experience before our life-changing encounter with the Lord's mercy. In the preceding stage, the goal of temptation is to prevent us from claiming the cornerstone of our faith through an authentic, all-embracing experience of forgiveness. Instead in this second stage, temptation's goal is to make us abandon the paths we have undertaken or return to the dispositions and ways of life we had before our regenerating experience of merciful love.

The famous eight capital vices,[1] upon which hinge the temptations in following Christ, continue to crop up in our lives. However, the enemy no longer presents vices in the same way as he would to someone less advanced spiritually or to a beginner on the path of spirituality. All temptations can be reduced to these eight vices and the queen of these is *philautia*, self-love. These temptations are disguised in a spiritually positive light so that what, per se, is negative in the vice is accepted thanks to its positive, or spiritual, trappings. Vainglory, for example, can be transmitted by the enemy into apostolic zeal.

In the following pages I will try to describe some temptations that at first glance could seem a single reality. In fact, my intention is precisely that of tracing the lines of some temptations and illusions that, in themselves, are very similar, because I want to call attention to the fact that in following Christ the spiritual path becomes refined, subtle. Nuances and details are important. Moreover, it is obvious that self-love and the love for one's own will are at the origin of all the problems in one's spiritual life.

The Schism Between Faith as Relationship and as Content[2]

I will now try to present the most frequent ways in which the enemy tries to lead one astray at the beginning of one's following Christ. The enemy's purpose is to make one stop on one's path and return to the attitude one had before one's experience of forgiveness and healing. The enemy would like, in some way, to make the forgiveness and salvation that God has wrought (2 Pt 2:17–22) count for nothing, but he cannot do so by proposing a banal, crude selfishness typical of one who is at the beginning of the path of purification. For he knows that persons whose hearts are warmed by Christ and his love no longer want to return to who they were before having consciously received salvation and life in the Holy Spirit. He knows that to try to force them to do so is practically impossible. So the tempter attacks these persons in such a way as to make them return to assuming the *attitude* of sin—that is, the attitude of people who rely on themselves, are preoccupied with themselves, and are moved by a passionate self-assertion. He needs to do so, however, with thoughts that seem to fit within each person's spiritual world. The enemy will very gradually lead these persons away from the paths they have been walking so they are no longer truly with Christ although they think they are. Christ will cease being a living person for them, no longer the Lord and Savior. Conversing with him will be substituted with thinking about him, even with meditations on dogma and doctrine, or, perhaps, with an intense feeling that seems to be for him.

In reality, however, these people become locked once again in their own egos, and their Christ is a fantasy. Under the influence of the enemy they will become involved with projections of themselves, but with the

> The attitude of sin is the attitude of people who rely on themselves, are preoccupied with themselves, and are moved by a passionate self-assertion.

mentality of sinners, of unsaved, unredeemed persons. He will make them seem to be living in Christ, while in reality they will be living without him. He will make them seem to believe, while in fact they will not even be in relationship with God. The enemy must in some way make the salvation won by Christ useless while keeping the persons within a religious system, with religious desires and aspirations of holiness, but with the mentality of sin, that is, living like those who have never met Christ and been freed from the slavery of self-love.

With his deceptions, the enemy moves from realism to illusion, from love to isolation, from life to the desert, from being saved to not being saved. We become religious but without God—or perhaps with our own god, a god reduced to whatever made our former selves comfortable—while we believe and are convinced that we are spiritual. We can even succeed in convincing ourselves of our holiness and perfection, but without conversion. Or we might believe we're converted simply because we changed a detail in our lives. The enemy will do everything to keep us from being truly reached by love so that we will not open ourselves to love or commit ourselves to love, but simply think we have.

The enemy's main goal is not to attack God, but to attack the love of God. The tempter will try to detach the person from a true, spiritual environment, from an ontology of agape, of love. There are actually not many temptations regarding God. The word "God" is too abstract and lends itself to infinite manipulations ranging from abstract intellectualism to sensory or psychological ritualism. That is why, to be effective, the temptation regarding God must touch what God really is: love (cf. 1 Jn 4:8).

First, it is helpful to understand the tactics of the enemy—step by step. God is the communion of Father, Son, and Holy Spirit. In history, this God of love reveals himself as a paschal God, that is, as the sacrifice of himself, as death and resurrection. The enemy will do everything possible to discredit God's love so that we don't believe in its truth and absoluteness. He wants us to reject the path of love—that is, the paschal path—and doubt that the "death" of self-sacrifice brings life. The enemy empties the path of Christ.

Second, it could be that we become enthusiastic about the newness we have experienced in Christ, about the newness of encountering love, so much so that we talk about it, and talk about it a lot, taking on more and more of the Christian experience, becoming increasingly more popular and important in religious circles, but always more in the manner of our old selves. The goal of the enemy's action is always to break us away from love. To believe in God means to recognize him as he is, and this means loving him.

Third, in the ecstasy of love, we are called to recognize God in everything he reveals to us. We recognize his Face, but also what this Face says and communicates. Believing in God also means loving what God says of himself, that is, the content of faith. The enemy tries to divide our relationship with God and the content of his revelation, our belief in God and the objective, articulated reality structured by faith, though these are actually inseparable. The tempter pits one against the other, toying with us in one or the other area. He either appeals only to God, to Christ, to the Holy Spirit in a subjective, charismatic way, negating any objective, historical dimension incarnated by the faith, or he reduces the objectivity and content of the faith to systems of concepts, precepts, or institutions separated from the living Person of Christ, detaching the content from the Face. In either of these positions we are essentially no longer believers because in reality we are alone, isolated from a true communal relationship, without that relational attitude of agape and style of life that God communicates to us together with an awareness and knowledge of himself.

Fourth, the enemy can work in us so that faith is reduced to an ideology by which we manage our lives on the basis of good intentions, lofty thoughts, and values with high moral content. Inevitably, however, day after day, we see the gap widening between our thoughts and our lives. We begin compromising, lowering our ideals to match our behavior. Faith is reduced to a mere ideal-moral world, and a rift is created between faith and life. When this happens, faith no longer has any point.

Life flows through relationships, and faith is an affirmation of the primacy of relationship and communion on both a divine and human level. That is why faith always favors life and communion. Faith reduced to an ideology, even if it is dressed with religious vocabulary, betrays itself with its sterility because it does not produce communion and does not create community. This is not faith in the Christian sense.

When we are touched by God and come to know him as Savior, God then also communicates to us a way of living, that is, a resemblance to him, as we saw in Part I. The awareness we have of God transforms us. It changes us because it is a relationship in which the Holy Spirit works in and with us. We know God because he relates to us. God saves us by giving himself to us. It is God's gift that makes us similar to him, because it radically unites us to his love. Faith in God gives us a style of living and a mentality that grows in spiritual awareness. In this way a culture grows that is ever more strongly permeated by the gift received from God. If, instead, the enemy succeeds in leading us into a rift between God's Face and the content of faith, then the divorce between culture and the Gospel will grow wider and more serious. The cultural question, therefore, is mainly a spiritual question, a question of the spiritual life.

Sensuality[3]

When a person feels a warmth within because of a felt connection to the Lord, especially during prayer, the idea may come to the person of making some sacrifice for God. Through this sacrifice the person hopes to show the Lord the responsibility with which he or she has accepted his gift. Perhaps it is intended to help him or her respond to God with more energy and determination. The person chooses some ascetical practice (prolonged prayer, fasting, some sacrifice or self-denial, etc.). Often the person feels a certain spiritual joy as a result, an authentic inner light that makes him or her feel much consolation.

Slowly, however, the enemy can introduce thoughts that lead us off the path. We might begin to focus a lot of attention on this inner warmth, on this pleasant light that gives such satisfaction. We feel very consoled as we stay with the experience in prayer. Very gradually, certain thoughts begin to gel, becoming more defined, more precise, revolving around one or two things. These thoughts become more insistent and confront us with challenging questions.

The questions demand an answer, a commitment, and immediate decisions. We feel flustered, pressured, and confused by the sudden urgency to do something right away. We are tricked so easily into dialoguing with unsettling thoughts. We grow assertive and zealous about these issues, but in such a way that we become the protagonists of the actions we decide to carry out. There is a subtle passage from an authentic sensation of spiritual warmth and zeal to protagonism in our spiritual struggles: we are the ones engaging ourselves.

With people of a weaker, less creative, and open-minded character, the enemy adopts a contrary tactic. Through an inner light he attracts their attention, making them follow him, inspiring thoughts of abandonment, of stillness, of not doing anything, not wearing themselves out too much. Instead, he shows them the value of prayer, of silence, and of abandonment to the pleasant state that accompanies these thoughts. Gradually, such people decide that spiritual struggles no longer make sense, are no longer important; it is enough just to enjoy salvation. The enemy deludes them into thinking that the well-being they have achieved is what it's all about. Without their realizing it, the thoughts that are presenting themselves to them are no longer spiritual. How can this happen? When our hearts are warmed and enflamed by the Lord, both the Holy Spirit and the enemy spirit can "blow on the fire," but each does so for a different purpose: one to draw us closer to Christ, and the other to draw us away from Christ, that we might be wrapped up in ourselves and at the service of our own wills. This is why we pray, participate in the liturgy, and give alms with attention and sobriety, careful not to be hooked by feelings and "spiritual" experiences. At the beginning of a spiritual journey we risk praying more for an immediate psychological effect than for building a

> When our hearts are warmed and enflamed by the Lord, both the Holy Spirit and the enemy spirit can "blow on the fire," but each does so for a different purpose.

relationship with God. When we seek warmth, well-being, sweetness, and peace in prayer and our other spiritual exercises, the enemy is all too able to enter the door of our expectations, to respond to our desires, presenting us with images of ourselves, of our spiritual lives, of God, of the saints, that feed our emotions and feelings and occupy our minds. The tempter's purpose is to sell us on his thoughts and make us reason according to his plan. Since we are enamored by some of the spiritual journey's psychological effects and begin to expect them, the enemy procures them for us in order to capture our attention and then, slowly, direct us toward his real intent.

Whoever walks the path of the *sequela Christi* must be very clear that in itself no exercise of spiritual devotion carries weight, but is only a means to acquiring the life of God through the Holy Spirit in order to strengthen one's participation in God's love. It is not helpful, therefore, to get overly excited about any of the formalities of the spiritual path; rather, temperance should be the rule. What then should be done with one's imagination? Many spiritual masters, precisely because of the deception that can hide behind a rich and full imagination, suggested a spiritual journey without images and without imagination. It is enough to think of Evagrius Ponticus or, in the West, of the Carmelite school of prayer. Use of the imagination in prayer is eliminated precisely to safeguard the person from the deceptions just described.

There are, however, many other spiritual authors who have not eliminated the use of the imagination, but suggest instead that we examine it in order to avoid the enemy's snares (for example, Diadochus or Ignatius of Loyola). How should we go about doing this? Observe the parade of thoughts and feelings in prayer and in spiritual moments of great warmth and intensity. If, at the beginning, throughout, and at the conclusion of prayer, the thought remains oriented toward the Lord in order to make us more Christ-like, to give him more precedence, and to open us more to him, then the warmth and light are spiritual. We should observe the sentiment in the same way: if at the beginning, in the middle, and at the end it orients us toward the Lord and enflames us for him—as the Lord is presented by the Word of God and the Church—then the thoughts that accompany such feelings are spiritual. If we discover, however, that at the beginning the thought seems to lead us to God, but by the end it has inclined us toward ourselves, inciting worries or giving rise to protagonism or pleasant resignation, then the imagination has been blown upon by the enemy.

It helps to test one's thoughts, talking back to them in precise and brief responses. This is the method that the Fathers called *antirrhésis* (talking back), in the example of Jesus who, tempted by the devil, answered by citing Scriptures without entering into discussion with the Evil One (cf. Lk 4:1–12). One's response, however, must be absolutely oriented toward Christ. It must have Christ as its object and be about him. One's response must show that the enemy is not really capable of giving anything that has not already been given to humanity with the death and resurrection of Christ. One's response must either make the enemy admit to being incapable of giving anything, or show him one is interested in nothing other than a powerful union with the crucified and risen Christ. Examining one's thoughts and feelings will make one more authentic in one's relationship with Christ. Illusions and false imaginations are conquered by the realism of a relationship with him.

The enemy creates fantasies about the things of God, holy things, holy persons, or even ourselves and our spiritual future, to fool us in three ways: to become the protagonists of our spiritual lives by desiring satisfaction above all, to make us content to stay "on the way" because it is so satisfying, or to give us such intense feelings that we think we have attained the height of sanctity.

The enemy can work on one's imagination so that one fantasizes about spiritual practices or even a religious vocation in an earthly—that is, sensual—manner. One can imagine that one is deeply spiritual, receiving many satisfactions and pleasure in the total absence of suffering, sorrow, and failure, completely outside the paschal dynamic. On the other hand, the enemy can arouse in other people great satisfaction when they imagine themselves as victims, as persecuted and suffering, etc. In any case, the conclusion is always the same: by seeking the pleasurable, the satisfying, or the sensual within a spiritual exercise, one becomes the protagonist of one's spiritual life.

Attachment to One's Own Mission[4]

For one maturing in the Christian life, the enemy will set traps under the appearance of zeal. He will tempt one to concentrate more and more on the good that one does, one's mission, and the works one carries out. The enemy will point out how successful one is in the Lord's service. Gradually, one unconsciously begins to feel that the service one carries out is important, and one begins to feel attached to it. One feels responsible to the point that one cannot live without it.

This attachment seems, at first glance, to be for the mission and the good that "must" be done, but, in fact, it is an attachment to one's own satisfaction, to the pleasure one derives from one's work. This is also a form of sensuality, a form of self-love. People with such an attachment fiercely defend all the good they are doing. Out of a moralistic idealism they may even promise complete availability and show an attitude of almost exemplary obedience, but in reality, as soon as things do not go as they plan or want, they start to feel bad. Even if they did not run into obstacles, sooner or later the truth of their self-love and passionate, sensual attachment to personal satisfaction and being in charge would come out. Pretexts for justifying their activity rest almost always on the amount of good they have done and the success they have had, which demonstrates how deceived they are by the enemy.

People who have a strong character can actually convince themselves that they and the work they do are indispensable to others, and, in a fundamental error, indispensable even to God. As can be seen, even the good one does can be obscured by the enemy when one unites it to a need for satisfaction and approval. Even as one continues doing good the enemy draws one's gaze away from the Lord and back to oneself. In one's zeal for the Lord and for serving him, one is continually mindful of oneself: How do I feel? What am I experiencing? Are people accepting me? How am I getting what I want?

Though one's zeal is apparently for the Lord, in reality it is characterized by an attitude and mentality of sin, that is, the mentality of the old self.

A second way the enemy can tempt us at the beginning of the spiritual journey is by impelling us in our enthusiasm and apostolic zeal to make ourselves teachers of others prematurely. As soon as this happens, the enemy sets in quickly so that we carry ourselves with a certain seriousness, praying, pondering, and loving these spiritual realities as if they were a weight, but at the same time we're teaching and communicating these realities in a rushed manner. We assume a role that the enemy turns into a prison. We convince ourselves that we are spiritually enlightened and able to teach others, but from that point on we cannot give ourselves the smallest spiritual counsel, because the enemy has made us spiritually illiterate through a false knowledge. In this way we come to a fundamental error in the knowledge we have of ourselves. The enemy has induced in us, through urgency with which we set about doing the good, false self-images and self-ideals that are actually confirmed by the people to whom we feel sent. Thus the advice we give out is based on the images we have accepted of ourselves, images that are false.

In time we begin to feel bad because our spiritual lives begin to decline and we see ourselves leading lives of illusion. The enemy does everything possible to keep us from digging up anew the truth as to how we stand before God. The deception, however, is clear from the fact that we feel misunderstood precisely by those closest to us, who are guilty of not understanding our greatness, our preparation, our gifts, that is, of not seeing us as temptation has made us see ourselves to be. The discrepancy highlighted by such relationships reveals the deception.

The exact opposite could also happen, as often did with the saints. They could have been true masters of the spiritual life, sought out by many and with long lines of people waiting to speak to them, but their closest brothers or sisters belittled them. The truth of this spiritual state was revealed in these persons' paschal attitude. They entered into suffering knowing that their passion was not prepared by them alone, but often by those closest to them. In fact, these saints were strengthened in their faith by the Lord, who sent them the Consoler so that they might not only die but also rise as persons of peace bearing the face of mercy.

Thinking One Is God's Executioner[5]

When one radically surrenders to Christ, one's attention can become concentrated on some specific behavior or way of thinking: for example, obedience, orthodoxy, chastity, some concrete practices, or a particular theological-spiritual school.... It is as if one wanted, through this thing, to express one's will to follow the Lord. Perhaps the person even experiences such a behavior or manner of reasoning as a particular grace.

The enemy takes advantage of this exaggerated focus and begins to draw one's attention to the attitudes, thoughts, and behaviors of others that are strikingly different from one's own. From the moment I associate this behavior with adherence to God, I think that others who do not do or think the way I do are not living spiritual lives. Before I realize it, I unleash a "holy war" against those who do not live the way I believe they should. The enemy has made me the criterion of judgment on who lives or does not live the faith and of how acceptance of the Lord is or is not lived. I hand down predominantly ethical-moral sentences against a religious backdrop for everything that happens under my gaze.

When the enemy influences me in this way, playing on my sensitivity to moral judgment over others' attitudes and behavior, he pushes me toward making reparation for them: I dedicate myself to prayer, long vigils, and penitence for those who do not have, as I see it, the right attitudes and actions. Oddly enough, however, despite the abundance of prayer, my verdict on the others is unimpeachable; it never changes. Rather, the enemy, true to character, pushes me even further so that though I cry out in prayer for the errors of others, I end up becoming an "executioner," and no one can speak about life's events or something that has happened in the world, or express a simple opinion, without this tendency appearing in me.

Such people always speak "ex cathedra," with unshakable certainty, and without perceiving the harm of their dogmatic words. The enemy has succeeded in moving them from a spiritual attentiveness to an attitude that no longer has anything spiritual about it because it has betrayed humility and love. The steps along this slipping away of consciousness, however, were not trivial. They were always wrapped in the mystique of reparation, compassion, and sorrow for the world. This "world," however, was reduced to a specific group of people, to a restricted area, or else it remained completely abstract because the people who sat in judgment were dominated by an absolutely blind judgment, completely detached from mercy and love, and had closed the door to a relationship with God and others. This is a mechanism that the tempter uses very frequently, above all in our cultural climate where the ethical-moral component has become more powerful.

Third, the enemy has another mechanism, similar to the one just described. In this case, one begins the journey of surrender to Christ, yet understands the enthusiasm of following the Lord solely as an intellectual system, a structure of thought that strictly binds one to this path toward the Lord. Just as in the previous mechanism the enemy proposed a particular attitude or behavior as indispensable, an index of the complete truth, a criteria by which to judge the actions of others, so now he isolates a few truths in a precise verbal, conceptual, or formal formulation and makes them seem to the person absolutely indispensable, the condition for any real step in faith. The enemy focuses one's attention on some details to make one lose sight of the whole. One begins to evaluate everyone's way of speaking and thinking on the basis of these fragments, which are nonetheless considered to be the whole picture.

When faith becomes an ideology we do not realize how quickly the chasm between ourselves and Christ and his doctrine grows. The enemy succeeds in separating the doctrine of Christ from love, but also in presenting it as something distinct in itself. "If you love this doctrine, it is necessary to fight for it—or better, in the name of it." This is obviously a subtle game to separate faith from love. The tempter makes us feel zealous and very religious, makes us feel close to Christ, and, precisely because of this closeness, impresses on us the duty to fight in the name of specific teachings or ideas. It is to fight for Christ, but not in the way of Christ. Ideas become idolatrous, and it is possible to confuse faith with specific schools of thought, even certain methods. A real bond to Christ, the Savior of humanity, is lost. There is no longer any living experience of saving love, yet we judge ourselves to be like Christ and committed to the work of salvation. The enemy succeeds in getting us to believe that an idea about Christ is more important than Christ himself, more important than persons and their lives. In this way the tempter shatters the Christian life. Virtue disintegrates. We defend the values of a certain sector of moral life and without any concern whatsoever rudely trample on those of another. We don't even realize the danger of what we're doing, because the value we are defending has completely taken over our relationship with God and we believe we are justified in what we're doing, even worthy of merit. There is no possibility for growth or change if we think our actions are praiseworthy and pleasing to God. The logic of the imperative sets in.

What is most unfortunate is that the authenticity of the salvation we have experienced has been destroyed, just as the enemy had planned. Salvation is kept alive by a constant attitude of humility. We cannot forget where we were when the Lord found us. We remember the behavior and mentality from which we were rescued. Those who constantly nourish the memory of the Lord's coming to them to redeem them will naturally have a benevolent gaze toward others. They know that if others had received the graces they had received, they would already be far more advanced in their spiritual lives. They keep in mind their former darkness and know that grace, a free gift, is a light that has been visited upon them, a light to which they could only respond. They therefore look with love and tenderness on those who in the cold and darkness still struggle to respond to grace.

Thoughts Conforming to the Psyche[6]

The tempter works in a subtler manner with those who have had a more powerful, intense, and total encounter with God, who walk decisively and safeguard the memory of God's love. He knows obvious tactics won't work with these people. So the enemy disguises himself, working on the psyche. He proposes thoughts specifically chosen to match a person's virtue. For example, the enemy inspires devout thoughts in the person who is devout, courageous thoughts in the courageous person, generous thoughts in the generous person, etc. The enemy is capable of pretending to pray with the person who prays, of fasting with the person who fasts, of doing works of charity with the person who is being charitable, all in order to attract the person's attention. He enters into one's house so as to make one go with him into his. There is a close relationship between the working of the psyche and the work of both the Holy Spirit as well as the tempter.

We have become who we are as a result of our histories, our memories, the education we have received, our cultures, even the environments and geographical contexts in which we have grown up. We understand, perceive, think, feel, and intuit with everything that we are. We are, on the one hand, our histories, our received heredities, and, on the other hand, our aspirations, desires, and tendencies. It is not just the intellect or reason that thinks, but the whole person; it is the human person who thinks, perceives, feels, desires, projects, and responds.

Authentic self-knowledge is paramount, and a true understanding of ourselves includes an understanding of the layers in our psychological memories, of their most active, powerful, painful, and sensitive points, in order to be more attentive to what thoughts come into our minds and where they can gain footholds. We need to maximize the experiences and develop the character traits that make us more cautious, prudent, and sharp in weighing our thoughts.

The Holy Spirit acts through all of a person's dimensions, keeps in mind all of his or her history and psychosomatic structure. The Holy Spirit knows a person's world better than the person does, both the world of the spirit as well as of the psyche and body. The enemy also knows this inner world and keeps it in mind. Just as the spiritual powers take us seriously in all our dimensions, so must we if we hope to respond to the Holy Spirit and unmask the deceptions of temptation. It is an illusion, by the Holy Spirit's logic, to think that psychological integration is necessary in order to live spiritually. The Holy Spirit speaks to people as they are, and Christ saves people as they are. God does not love the fantasies or idealistic projections we have of ourselves, precisely because these separate us from our truth and reality.

Psychology can help us understand ourselves, our histories, and our psychosomatic worlds. It can certainly help us work through many of our reactions, making them more peaceful, simpler, and less dramatic. However, this doesn't automatically make us more spiritual. It is possible to reach a certain psychological tranquility, but not, for all that, to grow in one's faith, love, and zeal for Christ. A psychology truly useful to my spiritual growth is one that accompanies me toward the integral mystery of my person and that includes what is fundamental in the world of the Holy Spirit—both of my person as well as of my psychology.

Moreover, an understanding of the spiritual world frees us from psychologism. In fact, a sort of psychological reductionism, insistent on the person's well-being, is incapable of giving value to suffering, sorrow, and imperfection. It can offer you a rational explanation at all costs for everything, teaching you how to avoid struggle, discomfort, and the like, deceiving you into thinking there is no longer a place for suffering, emptiness, neurotic tendencies, or fragility.

The Holy Spirit's logic, however, sees straight what we see as crooked, sees clear what we perceive as opaque. The Holy Spirit is capable of integrating even psychological suffering, transforming it into a spiritual value. It should never be forgotten that the vital principle for the body is the soul, and for the soul it is the spirit, and for the spirit it is the Holy Spirit. The force and sphere of integration is therefore the world of the spirit that reaches to the marrow of one's being. That is why it is necessary to have a knowledge of the spiritual world that is at least as profound and perceptive as the knowledge one has of one's corporeal and psychological world. One must learn the art of seeing how the Holy Spirit penetrates one's psychosomatic world, identify one's resistances, and explore what might support one's spiritual maturity.

The purpose of such a process is Christification, and the Holy Spirit moves each of us toward this. This likeness with Christ is not a question of taking on a preestablished form, but it is a mystery of agape and, therefore, a mystery of the paschal triduum. Only the Holy Spirit knows how the event of God's love is working even in people who are deeply troubled and suffering. A glimpse into the knowledge of this mystery is given to spiritual persons, since only spiritual persons can judge spiritual things. Psychological knowledge cannot substitute for spiritual knowledge. Nevertheless, a reciprocal dialogue between spiritual mystery and psychological knowledge, in the proper hierarchy, can more completely illuminate the mystery of the person.

As noted above, we need to remember that the enemy can't conquer the person who is very determined to live a spiritual life unless he enters into the intimate dimensions of the person, zeroing in on those areas that are most important to the person for one reason or another. The enemy will speak in that person's spiritual language and in conformity with his or her spiritual ideals. The second stage of discernment lies in this struggle. The enemy won't even tempt such persons with thoughts that are negative, ambiguous, or even explicit temptations. Instead, the thoughts the enemy suggests will fit in inconspicuously with what they have already established beforehand on their Christian journey. For example, to one who is full of apostolic zeal, the enemy will not suggest a thought of laziness or sloth, such as lounging around at home, minding one's own business, etc. The enemy knows that such a person won't even listen to suggestions like these. Instead, he will inspire the thought of offering oneself to the bishop for a mission, of entering into a very radical missionary order, of taking advantage of free time to visit people and speak of Christ and salvation. To others, the enemy will suggest the desire to make atonement as victims, or else to lock themselves away in a hermitage, to be rejected by all, and so on. Only suggestions like these would be accepted by such persons.

However, if this is not God's will, even the thought that seems the most holy, once accepted, causes such a person's spiritual life to decline in intensity and focus. In certain cases, the person might discover he or she is on the wrong path, one that is not for that person even if it is good in itself. When this happens, the person will be able to follow the Lord only with difficulty. His will seems too hard to accomplish. Finally such persons may lose themselves in their own wills.

In the second stage of discernment the enemy is very astute in tempting one who is progressing in the spiritual life. Often one is unable even to notice that one is falling into a "thought-trap." The person feels the idea woven, as it were, into his or her very being. The person embraces it with zeal and characteristic determination. The clue that this is actually a trap, however, is the insistence or obstinacy one feels about that thought.

Obstinacy is a symptom of that spiritual illness called *philautia*, "self-love," which often takes the form of love for one's own will. A spiritual person becomes aware of the snare precisely in the act of saying in prayer or to another person: "This thought is so *me*"; "This project is just perfect for me; it feels tailor-made"; "I just love this or that thing; it really expresses who I am"; "This is my choice...." It is precisely this accent on *"me"* that makes a spiritual person suspicious, for whether one likes something or not, or feels it to be one's own or not, really does not matter.

Another clue that one has fallen into the enemy's trap is defending a thought to the bitter end. Many ancient spiritual authors have put us on guard against insisting on a thought or defending it at any cost, supporting it with a holy intention or perhaps even with words from Scripture or the Church. They called this attitude *dikaioma*, the attempt to justify oneself so as to give oneself the illusion of being on the right path. They also considered it an index of self-love. In reality, though, I am defending this thought because it is not from God. The enemy is instigating me to fight for it, because he knows that it will otherwise come to nothing, since it is not from God. Thus, since it is my thought, if I don't defend it, no one will. It is for this reason that I defend it.

In the end, the most revealing indication that the thought is a trap is that, while I cultivate or express it, my gaze remains fundamentally oriented toward myself, and my interest becomes carrying out my own project or my own idea. God, who with his grace, his action, and his will wants everything to be done with the love that is realized in the passion, no longer has the first place. I might even initially have received the inspiration of a paschal thought, but the enemy is also capable of inspiring such a thought. I can recognize its true nature if I discover that after repeating it, pondering it, and praying with it my gaze is turned back upon myself, my self-assertions, and concern for myself.

One more indication of the enemy's work is exaggeration. An apparently spiritual thought, one oriented toward Christ and the good of all, can work itself out in such a way that I end up becoming isolated from others, from the larger picture, and from Christ. Although the thought seems so *me*, in reality, it is cutting me off from self-integration, and I begin to exaggerate one or another dimension of my life. I do the same thing with my relationships to Christ and others. I no longer maintain harmonious relationships or a vision of the whole, and I begin to concentrate my energies on something that in itself may be good, but which, little by little, makes me forget what others truly need or what radically characterizes the Christian life.

Exaggeration is always an attack upon unity, harmony, and beauty. When harmony is attacked, it is the heart that cries out. The heart, in fact, is the organ that safeguards the whole, the totality, the beauty of a person. The thoughts that arise out of disharmony slowly reveal themselves to be love for one's own will; they shatter inner unity and betray the very person. The Fathers said of *philautoi*, those who love themselves, that they are "friends of themselves who are against themselves." And so it is. I no longer love, but worry about myself. Then the heart, this organ that is attentive to the entirety of the person, has some serious self-examination to do. Has the unity and harmony of the whole been respected? Or am I like a body with the face of a child, the hands of an adult, and so on? Certainly each part of the body may be beautiful and elegant in its own right, but they do not hang together, they do not belong to the same person. Observing the thoughts that arise during prayer and along the course of my spiritual practices, I need to watch their development and make sure that they truly remain of the same quality, always inserted within the totality, within the entirety. I need to be aware if instead they deviate, falling into the isolation and disjointedness that are typical consequences for one who follows one's own will. In the beginning, I feel I am getting some benefit from doing my own will. Somehow I will be fulfilled. Always, however, I end up out of sync, an exile, a slave similar to the prodigal son who found himself tending pigs and starving.

According to Solov'ëv, love is the only absolute and personal reality because it unites everything that exists. To love myself means to see myself in the whole, as an individual together with humanity. To love myself means to see the connections that unite the different dimensions of my being, the different stages of my history, and the ways in which I am united with others. Self-love, on the other hand, those urgent thoughts of concern for myself and my needs, ends up in exactly the opposite place as authentic love. It ends in isolation and brokenness where I can no longer glimpse the living connections that create unity, a unity that alone is capable of calling forth happiness.

In people whose psyches have been wounded, the enemy continuously calls to their minds their weaknesses, vulnerabilities, and inabilities. He uses every means possible to keep their attention fixed on their sins. This is particularly painful for those who are truly reconciled with the Lord, in the Church. A dark force makes such persons continually concentrate on their sins, showing them in all their ugliness and gravity, in order to push these people into desolation and discouragement. The enemy may then play the card of false humility: "God could never forgive *my* sins." These people give more weight to their feelings than to the Church, which, praying over them, has explicitly affirmed that their sins *are* forgiven. The enemy wants us, in one way or another, to occupy ourselves with evil, but in a mistaken way.

> Many spiritual masters counsel us to remember our sins, but...a particular kind of memory of our sins...as assumed by the Lord and thus transformed into a memory of him who has forgiven us.

Many spiritual masters counsel us to remember our sin, but in an attitude of *penthos*, which, as we have seen, is a particular kind of memory of our sins—sins as assumed by the Lord and thus transformed into a memory of him who has forgiven us. This memory safeguards an attitude of sincere humility, which opens us to love and brings us close to God. The tempter wants us to attend to evil in a sensual way, enjoying it even though we shed some tears. If we conclude that we are not worthy to serve the Lord, to be with him, or to embrace a definitive choice for him in our lives, then we really are just asserting our own wills, a destructive and dangerous act. In dwelling on sins and the suffering they bring about, an unhealthy dynamic enters into our relationships with others involved in sin. We can weep, pronouncing ourselves unworthy, but in fact we are still accusing others, still pointing fingers. By emptying forgiveness of its meaning, the enemy slowly makes forgiveness impossible. We no longer feel the forgiveness God or others offer us, nor can we forgive ourselves or others.

The Temptation of False Perfection[7]

Another common temptation is that of false perfection. This is the enemy's tactic: he gives us temptations we can easily overcome, until we believe that we have become proficient at fighting temptation, avoiding the tempter's seductions, and overcoming difficulties with ease.

We then fall into a more dangerous trap: spiritual pride. It is not we who are able to defeat the Prince of Darkness, but God alone. It is the Holy Spirit who communicates the strength of the Lord of Light to drive away the darkness and defeat the tempter's deceptions.

The temptation is subtle; in the beginning, the enemy sometimes lets people overcome some temptations so they feel strong and good. The enemy can make those who can stand spiritual struggle and who live their

relationships with Christ with much joy, zeal, enthusiasm, and even a perceptible grace, believe the rich state
of their souls is their own doing, the fruit of their skill
and commitment, the result of their uprightness and
courage. Then without their realizing the progression of
the temptation, he plants in them the idea that since
they are good, know what to do, and are committed, the
Lord gives them this joy, this enthusiasm, this zeal. He
suggests: "It is obvious that the joy and enthusiasm you
feel is because you are good. You deserve it. You give,
you also receive."

A logic of commerce wins out, a logic of appease-
ment that is fundamentally self-appeasement. These
people believe they must have reached spiritual wisdom,
but their holiness is fundamentally self-satisfaction.
They consider themselves perfect and believe they are
experiencing truly spiritual joys. They feel they are
worthy of enjoying the fruits of their spiritual lives.

Once so self-deceived, these people are disturbed by
memories of others. From out of nowhere they
remember people who are angry with them or relationships that are not going well. Immediately they begin to
feel bad, to reconsider the relationships, blaming the
others for the way they feel. They themselves certainly
couldn't be to blame, for after all they are perfect. Their
thinking becomes obsessed as they try to figure out how
to fix *those* people, how to reprimand or change them. If
they have suffered unjustly at others' hands, the injustice
burns in their memories, and the offense is magnified.
How could they be treated so unfairly, they wonder.
After all, they are people of such great value and spiritual
depth. However, since the Gospel teaches that they must

forgive, they pray a great deal, even praying for those who have done them wrong. Yet despite their "forgiveness," they can't relate normally to the offenders. This is a sign they have not truly forgiven. Forgiveness is more than being particularly kind to someone who has hurt one. When one forgives, a relationship is brought back into balance because it is a relationship lived *in* Christ who gives himself to both parties in a conflict, who wants to save both. One's forgiveness is a participation in the forgiveness of Christ. This lack of forgiveness is precisely what begins to gnaw at those who presume themselves to be perfect. Since their spiritual lives are closed within their own small worlds, their faith is little more than a projection. Christ, the source of reconciliation, is missing between them and the other.

Even more, the "perfect" ones begin to feel a "call" to go to others in the role of "prophet," a call to conversion. They feel called to highlight the evils of others and point out what others should be doing according to their point of view. They swell with "spiritual" satisfaction because they do not see any need for their own conversion. Their perfection, which they humbly believe in—given that humility is a virtue that they "necessarily have to have"—leads them to isolation.

Perfectionists speak of compassion but are intransigent precisely with those toward whom they should have compassion, those who have wronged them. Those who presume themselves to be perfect are completely unable to see the injustice they have done to others. In the end, it is their perfection that prevents them from admitting they are capable of committing injustices against others.

Even here the enemy is so tricky; he shows them just a trace, a hint of some injustice they have done so that they feel even more perfect because they recognize this imperfection. Though they admit this "imperfection," they still do not recognize the real harm done and the faces of the persons they have wronged. They shed tears over some details of what they've done, while at the same time continuing to be harsh with others involved in the affair. It is as if they want to justify the way they behaved, and have even grown in virtue, since they have fought what appears to them to be enemies of God.

The "perfect" isolate themselves from those whom they think have wronged them, although they make a few the objects of their benevolence and forgiveness so that they can enjoy even more their "spiritual richness." Their manner of speaking, of throwing warnings around, and of playing a role, reveal their policy of keeping themselves apart, their attitude of superiority, and their creation of a black-and-white world in which they themselves are the center. Normally this false perfection ends in fanaticism. The tempter, taking possession of the reasoning of such person, invests them with special missions and vocations until they can no longer stop themselves and admit the illusions in which they find themselves.

The best medicine for preventing this tremendous temptation is the Church. No one chooses one's own church, one's own community, or one's own pastors on the basis of personal pleasure. Seriously living Church is the best way to overcome one's own subjectivism. It is the community, others, who actually help one to purify one's mind. Since what truly purifies is love—that is, charity—a constant exercise of charity helps to defend against this type of temptation. If we are able to maintain a certain peace despite discovering that others are working against us, speaking ill of us, or obstructing our work and our lives, we can be sure we are living in a dynamic of charity. Peace also implies not fighting back when others hurt us. Above all, not speaking ill of others foils the enemy's plans. As St. Maximus the Confessor said, speaking ill of others is a sin of laziness and of not maintaining purity of heart: if we have time to speak ill of others and to look for the wrong in them, we are not fulfilling our own vocations, the will of God, and therefore we have too much time. On the other hand, we only speak ill of others when we consider ourselves superior and have fallen into the trap of our own perfection.

Whoever dedicates a lot of time to maligning others is someone who is closed up in a little world, in the projection of his or her own perfection. Faith itself becomes part of this illusory world. Perfectionists do not go out of themselves toward others or even toward the Other who is God, but continue in worlds of their own creation, worlds of illusions. They might try to prove their perfection with iron-clad, logical arguments and explanations, but the simple fact that they dedicate themselves to pointing out the evil in others reveals false perfection. Moreover, it is the death of the spiritual life.

> Daily life for the truly perfect is lived in terms of death and resurrection.

True perfection is recognized by its christological and pneumatological dimensions and is rooted in the paschal mystery. Daily life for the truly perfect is lived in terms of death and resurrection, accompanied by a humility that makes it possible to bear peacefully the difficulties and trials of each day. Perfection does not consist in particular gestures or feats, but in the constancy of humility and paschal love. Daily tribulations are sufficient to prove true spiritual perfection. Whoever can bear such trials and tribulations with peace and serenity, by holding tightly to Christ, is spiritually mature. The most painful thorns in these daily tribulations are illness and the pain caused by those who are closest to us. These prepare the pasch for us.

Finally, an infallible criterion of true perfection is love for one's enemies. That is why spiritual writers teach the spiritual art of withstanding disgrace, humiliation, calumny, and injustice not with clenched teeth, that is, with self-control, but by drawing directly upon the Holy Spirit, who gives the Father's love and who alone is capable of transforming these sufferings and deaths into light and resurrection.

CHAPTER 6

How to Conquer Temptations

Spiritual Reading[1]

IN THIS STAGE OF SPIRITUAL GROWTH, spiritual reading becomes of fundamental importance. By spiritual reading I mean the reading of those texts truly steeped in the Holy Spirit that move us toward God, that bind us to God, that make us Christ-like, strengthening our spiritual reasoning and nourishing our spiritual taste. The writings of the great spiritual Fathers and Mothers of the Church's rich tradition are excellent for this reading. However, since these writings can be difficult to wade through unless one has had an introduction to them, a person can begin with the texts of authors who make the ancient tradition accessible to people today.

The text should be read with thoughtful attention, in such a way that we begin to dialogue with the writer. Understanding the writer's thoughts, we reassess our mentalities and experiences, noting where they correspond to or are supported by the writer's vision. In the same way, paragraph by paragraph, we highlight what is new and different for us. It helps to read a text more than once until it is well-absorbed and kneaded into our own ways of thinking, changing and transforming them.

Spiritual reading is not solely a mental exercise. It should lead us to make concrete choices: What does this text suggest regarding my experience? What newness could I begin to feel, to experience, both in my way of thinking as well as my behavior? It is helpful to ask ourselves: How does this reading illuminate what I have experienced up to now? How does it help me read my history with wisdom? How does it force my thinking to open up, helping me consider other realities or points of view and discover other connections and correspondences? Which of these thoughts could I adopt as my own?

Finding ourselves today deprived of spiritual imagination, we feel the powerful need to have before our eyes styles of living, anecdotes, images, and inspirations with which our creative imaginations can dialogue and create.

Other very important texts for spiritual reading are the lives of the saints. We moderns are often perplexed in the face of certain stories that obviously are not historically true. The ancient stories of the saints, however, were written according to the criteria of their times and for the purpose of nourishing the spiritual imagination. Only if we have an imagination are we creative, and the examples of the saints nourish our spiritual imagination, helping us develop this creativity. So many images, so many episodes, so many scenes from the lives of the saints have inspired those who read them. It is within this dialogical, inspirational, and creative principle that we correctly understand the "imitation of the saints." St. Cyril, apostle to the Slavs, was inspired to bring the Gospel to a new culture by St. Gregory Nazianzen, whom he had chosen as his patron saint. It is through friendship with the saints, speaking and praying in their company, that people are authentically inspired to imitate them. The anecdotes, legends, and inspiring images of the saints in any and every circumstance with which the ancients loved to fill their tales served to help spiritual inspiration. The morality of recent centuries, however, underlined the imitation of the saints in a direct, formal sense—obviously a course that risks depersonalization and an entire series of psychological and spiritual illnesses if not understood rightly.

Today, the invitation to imitate all these stories and rich images becomes a dangerous psychological game and has certainly raised a violent reaction to a moralistic and voluntaristic Christianity. Unfortunately in our more recent rationalist and positivist age, we have thrown out the elements of the episodes and legends from the stories of the saints that can't be historically proven. They have suffered the dry outcome of the application of the historical-critical method, with the result that the hagiographic tales have become almost illegible and useless.

Finding ourselves today deprived of spiritual imagination, we feel the powerful need to have before our eyes styles of living, anecdotes, images, and inspirations with which our creative imaginations can dialogue and create. We need more than abstract theories and ideas. Entire generations have been raised with imaginations fed predominantly on television, imaginations that are, as a consequence, mainly sensory, sensual, and carnal.

Even more, the youngest generations are exposed to the pervasive culture of the virtual image, in which digital culture creates an entire paradigm based on imagination that makes sensuality and sensory perception much more intense and total than that created by television.

Such a culture risks suffocating true and flavorful spiritual lives and certainly risks causing a crisis in vocations, be it to marriage, the priesthood, or religious life, since young people rarely choose paths that they do not see lived out in ways that convince them of the value of their choices. Only geniuses are able to create without an imaginative comparison to go by. Something even more serious can and already is happening. Because of a sort of "pendulum effect" that causes a unilateral tendency to be followed by an entirely contradictory one, a massive sensual imagination is provoking an idealistic, abstract, disincarnated, and ethereal religious reaction. Instead, the lives of the saints create these imaginative proposals against which we can compare ourselves, not in a formal, imitative sense, but in an "inspirational" way. The lives of the saints make us capable once more of creating.

What is more, a spirituality detached from the saints as living persons is very dangerous. A theoretical approach that gives precedence to the human sciences rather than to a life lived out in holiness is harmful to the spiritual life. As much as human science can help us, it is not able to reach the greatness of these people.

Finally, friendship with a saint is one of those things that can favor growth along a truly radical path. We choose our friendships on the basis of the sympathy we feel from others. A woman who is not happy with her husband, for example, will hardly choose to be with other women who are happily married and faithful to their spouses, rather she'll prefer the company of women who have a similar attitude to her own in order to find support and sympathy. In the same way we can see the importance in the spiritual journey of a network of friendships with persons who understand one another in the ecclesial community, on earth, and, above all, in the glorified Church in heaven. If charity marked the lives of the saints on earth, we can imagine the help they can offer to those who are their friends now and who call upon them for help.

Spiritual Dialogue or Direction[2]

As we have seen, the enemy disguises himself as an angel of light and enters one's spiritual world to draw one off the path and lead one once more to the life one had lived as a sinner before encountering mercy. In order to uncover his plots, it is useful to have a regular conversation with a spiritual person. In choosing this person, look for someone steeped in the Christian spiritual tradition who doesn't just speak on a theoretical level or do a lot of teaching when speaking with you, but someone who has truly encountered Christ and has personal experience on the path of life in Christ and with the snares that the enemy sets for us. We're not talking here about a friend or someone who will make you feel good. A spiritual guide puts one radically before the Lord, someone who has at heart only one desire: to serve the Lord and to assist the work that the Holy Spirit is already carrying out in one who has asked for spiritual direction. A good spiritual director sees how salvation is already being brought about in a person and supports a greater openness to redemption and the service of Christ so that his redemption may penetrate the world more deeply. In these spiritual conversations there is no investigation into the past. Rather, attention is given to that person's thoughts, intentions, projects, and desires. They speak together about that person's prayer, about what happens in prayer and how to proceed, because that is where the enemy lays his traps.

True spiritual dialogues are preventive medicine. Spiritual directors of this type are not very interested in personal histories, because they know that we all come from sin. They are interested in where we are going, what our aspirations are, what ideas we believe in, what thoughts we believe to be most inspiring, and so on. Revealing one's projects and inspirations to a spiritual person is like passing them through a filter. In this practice of discernment the thoughts instigated by the tempter grow weak and lose their force. Perhaps before the dialogue one was obsessed for weeks with an idea that set alight one's heart and enflamed one's zeal, but after having spoken about it with the spiritual director, it no longer has any hold or power.

Often spiritual directors "filter" these thoughts by being indifferent to them. If I am much taken with a thought, but my spiritual director doesn't seem interested or even passes over it in silence, I might feel bad. The thought's true nature is revealed to me by my very reaction.

It is also important to bring to these dialogues our relationships, not to analyze them, but to place in the light of day the influences and conditionings that come about through them so that we might better understand the action both of the Holy Spirit as well as of the tempter.

The Memory of God's Work[3]

Several times now we have seen how various spiritual authors strongly urge keeping alive the memory of what Christ has worked in one, continually recalling the memory of the foundational event, one's exodus from death. Just as the Exodus from Egypt became the foundation of the history of the Chosen People, and Christ's passion is the foundational event of salvation for the Church, celebrated in every liturgical act, so the Christian grows by recalling that aspect that has become his or her foundational event, that is, when and in what manner the Holy Spirit communicated the paschal mystery as his or her personal salvation.

In Part I, I spoke of *penthos* as a living memory of forgiveness. This *penthos* naturally develops into the contemplation of the Savior's Face. Remembering the benefits that God has worked in me and the graces I have received means constantly seeing the Face of him who bent over me, who called me forth from the tomb, who forgave me my sins, taking them upon himself. It is the contemplation of the Holy Face as a perennial memory of the benefits gained.

The Fathers believed that we become what we contemplate. For those who have consciously lived the foundational event—that is the Lord's passion—as the salvation of their lives, recalling Christ is not difficult; the lines and features of his Face are always more clear.

The thought of those who focus their attention on the Lord's Face is a thought that is ever alive and attentive because it contemplates life. It is a thought that cares for the other because it contemplates the other. It is unable to create or think in a depersonalized way. These persons walk secure, because the enemy does not find them lazy, inattentive, or lost.

Prayer in this second stage of discernment is the exercise of the memory of God, the exercise of invoking the name of the Lord as frequently as possible. It is a retracing of spiritual passages that have been read, repeating the words of Scripture, knowing they are full of the Holy Spirit. Prayer becomes simplified, detached from immediate, psychological effects, and takes on the aspects of an ever more mature relationship. We avail ourselves of powerful moments of encounter with God, such as retreats or spiritual exercises, or once a week, for example, we pray in a more structured way, using the method of prayer presented in Part I of this volume. This method of prayer is extremely important for seeing the development and process of our thoughts and feelings. When I spoke of the temptations of the enemy, I often said that it was necessary to observe whether our thoughts and feelings maintain their spiritual quality or get off course and end in self-absorption. Only the inclusion of a final examination in our prayer times offers us a consistent,

> The thought of those who focus their attention on the Lord's Face is a thought that is ever alive and attentive because it contemplates life.

effective method for verifying the course of our thoughts and feelings. This is why it is helpful to have a notebook in which to note the essential things that mature in prayer and in one's relationship with God.

The Church[4]

The tempter encounters a difficult obstacle when trying to tempt a Christian inserted into the Church. Christ is at the heart of the Church. Christ is recognized and celebrated by the Church as the Lord who offers himself, who saves us, and brings us back to the Father. In the Church, every act flows into the liturgy, into the worship of our Lord, true God and true man. In this worship, all of humanity is opened to the divine in Christ. In him, the absolute love of the Three in One opens itself to humanity. In the Church, through Christ, God makes his home among us, and in Christ we become children of God and his brothers and sisters, and we return with him to the Father as communion, as the image of the Trinity itself.

This mystery of the ecstasy of God, of his going out toward humanity, is celebrated in the Church's holy liturgy in which we worship our God and, at the same time, live our ecstasy toward him. This is why the liturgy has an "across time" dimension that draws directly upon Christ. The liturgy, therefore, must present and communicate in its language the objectivity of the christological dogmas that foster the truth of Christ. At the same time, however, the liturgy has a temporal and cultural dimension marked by human history, which must be respected. However, when a certain subjectivism prevails in the liturgy, it shows the weakness of the faith dimension because the subjective principle prevails over the ecclesial one. The objectivity of Christ, who is the liturgy's foundation, object, and purpose, begins to be clouded over and eventually lost all together.

What is essentially important in the liturgy for someone in this second stage of spiritual growth is the Christ who is celebrated there. A subjective catering to people's tastes and inclinations would undermine for them the Christ who is manifested and communicated, the Christ to whom we hand ourselves over. The Christian in this stage begins to reconstruct the relationship that has been dismantled between the eternal and temporal, between the objective and subjective.

This same attitude also begins to characterize my relationship with the Church. Less and less space is given to the subjective desire to create a Church in my own image, according to my own tastes; instead, I begin to feel the same tastes I experienced in my growing liturgical maturity. It is as if, in some way, I predominantly overcome a psychological and sociological approach. The theological dimension of my ecclesial sense is no longer theoretical but experiential, and I begin to feel myself part of the Church just as she is, with people who please me or not, with her concrete traditions, etc. I begin to feel *with* the Church.

Our lives in the Church began with Baptism. We feel as if we have been generated by the ecclesial community, born to a new life, and this determines a new way of experiencing the Church and of feeling ourselves part of the Church. The difficulties that the cultural, historical, and human dimensions of the Church can bring about become causes of suffering and of a sorrow that opens itself more and more to the paschal mystery. We have a realistic view of the Church. In this divine-human, transtemporal and historical realism of holiness and sin, of perfection and error, Christians live the paschal mystery. This paschal vision infallibly blocks temptations of the enemy. Thoughts that lead us outside this ecclesial realism, which either don't take it into consideration or avoid it altogether, are immediately recognized as traps.

Instructive Desolation[5]

Among the various stages that a spiritual person following Christ goes through, it is also important to underline instructive desolation. Instructive desolation, as Diadochus called it, is the moment when the Lord withdraws the sensible effect of grace from the human heart. In reality, grace remains, but its light and warmth are hidden. It is the Lord himself who allows the soul to be enveloped with a certain sadness and for the hour of temptation to arrive. The soul feels inconsolable, tepid, desolate. It feels a great weariness at each spiritual step. Prayer becomes difficult, the memory of God distant, and the saints absent. Foundational memories can no longer be recalled, and it is impossible to read Holy Scripture. When the person looks at the Church, he or she sees mainly the things that are wrong, and every possible obstacle shows up on the path. The person seems to have been abandoned by the Lord, but in fact this is not so. The presence of grace exists. God gazes on the person with love. Nothing can strike, wound, harm, or offend a person if the person does not lose his or her head but remains patient, invoking the name of the Lord without heeding the enemy's traps and the thoughts that arise from this affliction.

At this point the following rule is essential to remember: the enemy sows his thoughts in sadness, in affliction, and in desolation, and we therefore should not listen to these thoughts. Rather, we should be deaf to everything aroused in our souls and stay firm in invoking the help of the Lord and the saints. God allows us to pass through these deserts to animate those dimensions of our beings that still need salvation. God leads us to the edge of our possibilities and our strength in such a way that everything that we are is touched and used in invoking the Lord's name, in our thirst for grace, in the refusal to return to death and hell and the night of our faith.

> The Lord himself leads us into the desert so that we might learn to live realistically with ambiguous dimensions of ourselves.

On the other hand, there are dimensions of the spirit that we are not aware of precisely because our spiritual lives are going well enough and our hearts are on fire for God. There are aspects of our souls that are greedy for glory and, as soon as things start to go wrong, get discouraged and begin the decline that pulls us down. Then, the Lord himself leads us into the desert so that we might learn to live realistically with these ambiguous dimensions of ourselves. Here we need to be attentive that the enemy doesn't tempt us into believing we are already perfect, have already reached our goal. Through this school of desolation, we come to understand that tasting the sweetness of the Lord and the fervor of his presence are not given automatically. Growth often happens in the desert, in desolation, because it is there that our desires are purified.

The Lord allows this desolation to make it impossible for the enemy to lay in us his traps of perfection, of talent, of ease, and of independence. On one hand, we experience all the temptations typical of desolation, but because the Lord and his grace are in our hearts it is important not to listen to discomfort and emptiness; nothing bad can happen. In reality, however, at that very moment, the Lord is healing our more vulnerable areas, where the enemy can trigger thoughts of self-sufficiency, worthiness, and being able to save ourselves. The moments of such desolation are thus moments of grace, because they mature our relationships with God in such a way that we learn to follow the Lord not because he satisfies us sensibly with his grace, but out of love; not out of fear or convenience, but out of love. The Lord will send us instructive desolation for as long as we need it, until the risk of our thinking we can earn or buy his love—an attitude that leads us directly into the enemy's traps—has diminished to a minimum.

It is in the desert of such desolation that all consolations and compensatory pleasures, by which evil masquerading as an angel of light wishes to snag our hearts, are burned away. Undergoing these humiliations, we move toward the humility that recognizes that consolation comes only from God, from the Holy Spirit, and is a freely given, unmerited gift, far more precious and secure when it is completely unexpected. We learn to be cautious of associating too excitedly with thoughts or benefits or consolations. It is important to underline that desolation caused by the Lord for our good is character- ized by the absence of upheavals. The soul is desolate; it feels sad or empty, but it is not disturbed. A profound certainty that the Lord is there and that he will not allow us to return to our old lives remains.

Thought Without Cause[6]

Many spiritual Fathers consider the most spiritual thought to be the so-called "thought without cause." What does this mean? It is a thought that arises when one is not reflecting on spiritual things, not reading a spiritual text, not participating in a liturgy or living some event with any particular intensity. The thought that arises, then, is not a consequence or deduction from a preceding state or action that could have caused the thought.

A thought without cause is possible if the Lord dwells in our hearts, if we belong to him, if we have handed ourselves over to him, if we feel we are his and he can enter our hearts as if entering into his own room, moving the thoughts in our hearts whenever he wants. The Lord is the principle and the protagonist. Or rather, this Lord is the Holy Spirit who has free access to our hearts and can move our thoughts and feelings so that we recognize and live more completely our individual relationships with God. "Without cause," therefore, means "free." In reality, only God, the Three in One Love, is truly free. I enter into the process of liberation and feel free in virtue of the relationship I have estab- lished with God. The more I respond to this relationship, the more I open myself, the more this relationship makes me free.

A more creative example of this is the Gospel episode of St. Peter walking on water. According to his human nature Peter could not do that, but on the strength of his relationship with Christ, on the strength of his answer to Christ's call, he walked on the lake. His relationship was so strong that at the moment Peter was drawn to the Lord and rooted in his word "Come," he walked on the water.

> This Lord is the Holy Spirit who has free access to our hearts.

When fear arose from the wind blowing in his face and the darkness of the water under his feet, his attention slipped and he began to sink, returning to the logic of natural laws.

That which is "without cause" is the part of a free act that originates between two persons and that, thanks to the principle of agape, makes it possible for them to rise above the determinism to which they have grown accustomed. In this love that comes from God, determinism is overcome, and we live a sort of exodus from the laws of consequentiality and evidence, and our relationships are lifted to a higher level than previously possible. An example of this is St. Peter himself, who sought to stop Christ from undergoing the passion, whose human nature rebelled against the sorrow of his Master's coming death, who wouldn't even think of the defeat. It is this same Peter who will fully carry out the principle of agape, that is, God's love, in his human nature, culminating finally in his martyrdom.

From one side there is thus a movement from determinism toward a new standard of living, a new level of existence, and from another there is a return from this level of quality and its fulfillment to that natural world we are called to personalize, assume, and transfigure. A thought without cause is therefore a thought that comes from a free principle that attracts and involves one, and that is fulfilled in one's lived experience on the basis of a principle of free surrender. It is a thought of great spiritual quality that aims directly at life in Christ for one's good and the good of all. It is not violent, neither does it force itself upon one. On the contrary, it has no negative charge toward anyone. This thought arises freely and remains thus. It is a thought that appeals to one's free adherence, a free thought that makes one free.

When such a thought appears, it is helpful to be very attentive to how it develops, what paths it takes, and how it involves your reason and sentiment, because the thoughts that follow later will not necessarily be in line with it. Such a thought often warms your heart and illuminates your mind. You perceive you have had an intuition, and you quickly and easily begin to throw in your own thoughts, your own reasoning. To distinguish between the thought without cause, or original intuition, and the thought that follows, which originates from you, you need to be attentive to the dimension of freedom. If pressure and urgency show up in your reasoning, and you feel you "must" think or do something, you are already, beyond any doubt, out of the original thought. At this point it is best to return to the original intuition, hold on to it and immerse yourself in the feeling of freedom that accompanies this thought without cause.

The enemy will do everything he can to enter your mind and grab hold of a spiritual thought, because such thoughts totally escape him. They are outside his plotting precisely because of their free origin, since he, the tempter, as the perversion of agape, is by definition not free. Everything that is free is outside his reach.

In short, the method above can help us identify the feelings and thoughts born of temptation or, vice versa, those born of spiritual inspiration that show us how to respond to God's will, how to reason as saved persons, and how to move as redeemed persons within our world and our culture. By following the thoughts that are recognized as good and going along with them, the Christian grows in the fulfillment of his or her vocation in the world.

CHAPTER 7

Testing Our Free Surrender to Christ

"Sons in the Son"[1]

THE REDEMPTION CHRIST HAS WON for all humanity, and that the Holy Spirit reveals to each of us in a personal way by communicating to us Christ as our personal Lord and Savior, unites us with him in such a radical and absolute way that we feel we are the Father's adopted children. We rediscover ourselves as "sons in the Son." The Second Person of the Most Holy Trinity, the Son who fully possesses the whole of the divine nature assumes and therefore possesses human nature because of his incarnation. Since human nature is what belongs to the human persons who possess it, it cannot be an abstract, generic, or faceless human nature. Thus when Christ as the Son of God assumed human nature in the incarnation, he incarnated in it an absolutely personal source of love. He thus established a real and completely personal relationship with each human person who exists because each one possesses human nature.

The human person on the other hand is this insepa-rable unity of the nature proper to all beings that participate in it *and* a personalizing love that possesses that nature in a way that makes it a unique, unrepeatable, unmistakable person with a totally personal face. Assuming human nature, Christ possesses it as the Son of God. He thus brings human nature back to the truth it had in itself from creation, and at the same time makes into adopted children human persons who possess the same nature he has assumed. When Christ assumes human nature, he establishes such an intimate, personal, and complete relationship with the human person that this person becomes an adopted child of God.

Against this christological-anthropological background, one's spiritual journey clearly becomes an ever-greater surrender to the Son of God in order to give one's human nature an ever more integral imprint as God's child. This is our life in Christ: Christ makes us children of the Father, and the Holy Spirit given to us cries out in us "Abba," uniting us to the Son, and making us conscious of our relationship as children (cf. Gal 4:6–7). This gift causes us to hold fast with everything we are to Christ's work, which molds our human reality to his image, that is, as Son. We are created in the image of the Son.

With sin came about the perversion of the principle of agape—that is, the filial principle—in that we, created as sons and daughters, became rebellious, making ourselves the center of everything and everyone, refusing our status as children. Instead of being continual references to the Father, sin made us self-assertive, feeling ourselves to be creators in whom everything must converge and on the basis of whose wills everything must be run. Christ's salvation, through his death under the weight of sin's consequences and his treatment by sin, consists precisely in making us reenter the path of the prodigal son. He wholly assumes the catastrophe and destiny of rebellious humanity and opens the way for a true filial relationship with the Father, and thus for our return to him.

On the spiritual journey it is necessary to see how and to what degree we are adhering to Christ's love, how and to what degree we are opening ourselves to the action of the Holy Spirit who makes us like Christ. Thus the spiritual journey makes us ask, "How alive is the awareness of my belonging to Christ and being a child of the Father in him? Or how much, instead, does Christ remain a far-off ideal to imitate, a Master to follow, a God to adore, but in a purely external way?"

> The spiritual journey makes us ask, "How alive is the awareness of my belonging to Christ? Or how much, instead, does Christ remain a far-off ideal to imitate?"

It is one thing to *perceive* ourselves to be in Christ, to be "sons in the Son" who seek, with the Holy Spirit, to understand how to live as children of the Father and how to make evident the fact that we are rooted in Christ and that Christ lives in us. It is another thing to *stand* before Christ, admiring him, becoming enthused about him, listening to his teaching, trying to live what he asks, and even asking him to help us carry out what he teaches. Here a possible trap arises from not paying enough attention to the Holy Spirit. For by adoring and invoking the Holy Spirit, we give ourselves over to synergy, and our faith then has an ontological basis. Otherwise, we make faith something of an ideology with willful and moralistic outlets. For example, we can ask Christ to help us work and fight for justice, but as a sort of political "program." Those who have a Spirit-filled foundation, instead, know that Christ *is* justice, that he carries it out, and that we participate in Christ-Justice through the Holy Spirit. If we are called to work for justice, we know that it is already fulfilled in him and that our call in history is to live the justice that is Christ, in Christ's way. The Holy Spirit makes us participate in Christ in a manner that, fighting for justice, we fight as Christ does, in a way that makes Christ shine through. Without the Holy Spirit, we can invoke Christ, having his name always on our tongues, make reference to values, and attempt to create a program that bears his stamp, but none of these efforts will be participation in him. Consequently, Christ will not show through in the proposed values or in the implementation of projects.

There is an awareness of the dynamic connection of all the virtues when we operate within the sphere of the Holy Spirit. Every virtue is the path to another. Therefore, it is not possible to be just *and* violent or peaceful *and* unjust at the same time. This awareness eliminates the risks of an ideological Christianity, of a faith reduced to a willful and moralistic program with values that cancel each other out.

Testing One's Way of Thinking[2]

Macarius the Great noted that we can be chained by visible *and* invisible shackles, and that even if we can rid ourselves of the shackles that are visible, believing ourselves to be free, we may still be in a state of slavery. What are the most difficult chains to unlock? Many spiritual authors agree: freeing oneself from one's own way of thinking. Daily one might easily find very generous people who are ready to help in many ways, but it is difficult to find someone who is capable of thinking with others, of letting them speak, of having an open mind, that is, an authentically religious mentality. One could possess a whole list of Christian religious values, a way of thinking that rigorously follows the catechism, and continually cite the Word of God, encyclicals, documents of the Church, etc. But this still does not mean one is actually released from one's own way of seeing things.

Being tied to one's own thinking means having a way of thinking that is fundamentally—even if nobly—sensual and disordered. This mindset is capable of creating a mammoth intellectual system for protecting a small point—and it could actually be a vital point—but one is actually protecting one's own desires above all. It is this passion for one's own desires, this self-love as a unilateral assertion, that makes one's way of thinking sensual. From this it is clear how important it is to test one's way of thinking to see if it reflects the Gospel and adheres to Christ's way of thinking. Even if it does, one must go on to examine if it consists only in formal comparisons, that is, testing if, for example, one's way of saying things is limited to the words of the Gospel, the official declarations of the Church, or the founding saint of one's Order, and so on. Or rather, can one think about anything in life or history—be it one's own, society's, or the Church's—rooted in a spiritual freedom that prevents the spark of self-love from being struck?

This testing requires that I be particularly attentive to my reactions when, for example, I am treated unjustly by someone and I discover that others have spoken ill of me, when an economic or social injustice is done to me and I risk losing something important, when my health begins to falter.... These are all circumstances that reveal better than others whether my way of reasoning has a spiritual foundation and I am completely surrendered to Christ, or whether my foundation is passionate, sensual, and follows the world's logic (in the sense of John's Gospel). On this latter foundation, it is possible to build a structure with all the appearances of Christian perfection for the sole purpose of defending a passionate, hidden attachment. For this reason, it is necessary to determine if I have a way of thinking that can serve me on the journey to true life or one that leads us to an illusory life where I think *I* am sovereign, but am actually isolated. Isolation is the sign of death, because life only exists in love, that is, in relationships, in communion.

From deeply rooted sin emerges a way of reasoning that seeks to avoid the paschal triduum in my life. Sin was annihilated by Christ's cross, but the way of thinking characteristic of sin does everything possible to keep me from accepting the paschal logic, thus remaining in sin. In order to get me to avoid the paschal path, sin must show me that Christ's passion is not a sufficient argument for *my* passion, that Christ suffered the passion and died, but that passion is not the obligatory, archetypal route for me and my life. Rather, I need to work on saving myself, and that means, above all, avoiding the paschal triduum in my life. Salvation, however, comes *only* from Christ's passion, no matter how vigorously the mindset of sin tries to convince me otherwise.

The path to true life follows the journey of the paschal Christ, while that of sin tries to convince us that any other path is fine as long as it avoids the passion. Temptation can make this much more subtle: some people, because of their psychological structure or personal history, choose the path of the cross, abnegation, and suffering, but without the resurrection. This is a sort of "self-assertion" through pain and suffering. In this way, the mindset of sin succeeds in making such people use even suffering, pain, and defeat to affirm themselves.

In the contemporary world and culture there are many stimuli that encourage a "mentality of sin." We live in a culture characterized by the assertion of the individual, resulting in very particular lifestyles. Ours is a culture that, on the one hand, is governed by economic and financial laws that aggressively pit us one against another, but which, on the other hand, makes us fall prey to wanting to be "in style, in vogue." These cultural realities, together with many others, feed a self-centered style of reasoning, while a spiritual style of reasoning has been so marginalized that it becomes difficult to reason according to its criteria, even for persons who are very serious about spirituality.

Testing our way of thinking, in the spiritual sense, consists in seeing if we are able to understand that the path leading to true life is the paschal triduum of the Lord, a journey along which we will encounter misunderstandings, undergo disgraces, and be ill-judged on account of this Christ-like attitude, which some may consider unfounded and which may cost us everything we own, including consoling feelings that could nourish us along the Lord's path. Testing our way of thinking means seeing if we understand that the cross is the path to resurrection, or if we still think that, in order to make something of ourselves, it is necessary to assert our own ideas, to be successful, powerful, well-regarded, esteemed and applauded by all, healthy, rich, and endorsed from a social and economic point of view.

Nevertheless, one does not choose misunderstandings or disgrace. My part is to pray sincerely for God's grace so that, if it pleases God to put me on the paschal path, if it is for my salvation and truly for my good, I might be able to live this path and accept that my life is on this road. The thought of entering the paschal path is purified by my remaining free before the possibility of such a life. This unity between life and thought manifests the extent of my spiritual freedom and what underlies my choices. The unity between my ways of thinking and living can be based on either of two things: my own ideology and ethical principles, or on Christ who is a living Person. In Christ, this unity is fulfilled in an absolute way, but at the same time in a manner that I can participate in as a "son in the Son." It is the Holy Spirit who opens me to Christ's salvation, in which Christ assumes all of my reality and makes me the offspring of the Father. In this close relationship between myself and Christ—which is my participation in the Person of Christ—the Holy Spirit communicates to me Christ's unity of thought and life. I live in Christ, and in this unity of life and thought that is in Christ, I am able to know myself and become myself. Even more, the Holy

Spirit makes me feel that this unity of Christ's style of thought is indeed my own. If Christ is the foundation of my inner unity, then my actions and thoughts will not only have a high commitment and moral value, but will also be enlivened and sustained by Christ who is the foundation of my becoming who I am. This is the basis for the unity between the spiritual life and the moral life.

> The Holy Spirit communicates to me Christ's unity of thought and life, and in this unity I am able to know myself and become myself.

Finally, we can test our ways of thinking in prayer, contemplating Christ's life above all in the key of the paschal triduum, the passion and resurrection, continually testing the depth, readiness, and sincerity of our prayers to the Lord, asking that if it is pleasing to the Lord to give us the grace to live this paschal way, that he do so, because it alone leads to true life, since he is the Truth and the Life.

Testing One's Way of Willing[3]

We have just established the importance of spiritual freedom in one's way of reasoning, which deals with the human dimension that is most vulnerable to self-love. The second testing of one's surrender to Christ is the testing of one's will. Now, often after a strong purification or a true reconciliation, one's will feels ready for the struggle against sin and evil, ready to renounce the hidden traps of the tempter, and one might easily think oneself truly free, that is, completely disposed to doing good.

As we have already seen, however, the true snare laid by the enemy is that of self-love. It is therefore necessary to see if we still have the inner chains of a disordered attachment to our talents and virtues, that is, an attitude that is *apparently* completely disposed to fulfilling the will of God but which, in reality, pushes forward its own attachments and ties. We can be so attached to our good intentions, our projects, and our visions of the mission to be accomplished, precisely because they are so good and Gospel-oriented, that we don't notice that it has all become about our self-love. Self-love camouflages itself beneath attachments to good things and intentions, good ideas and projects.

It can happen that people who have such attachments can actually believe in surrender and complete detachment, because they know these are the only ways they can entrust themselves to God and build their lives on him. However, two things can go wrong. First, despite knowing that detachment is necessary, they make no move, do nothing to bring it about, and push the decision off until another day without using the means that Christian spirituality gives them to overcome attachments. Or they can pray for hours on end without praying in a way that helps them to become free. They can fast but in such a way that it doesn't help them grow in greater inner freedom. So they can either not use the means of Christian asceticism or else use them but not to their true purpose. Self-love holds them at a stalemate through a sort of sluggishness that impedes them from ever vigorously deciding to act against these attachments that get in the way of their total self-offering to God. Normally we convince ourselves with devout rationalizations or psychologize about our situations, persuading ourselves that we are already living good lives and doing more than enough to reach salvation.

Self-love plays yet another trick. People convince themselves that the Lord wants them to accept their attachments as if he were the one who willed them. They try to draw the Lord himself into their attachments instead of freeing themselves from them and going out to meet him. These people usually pray very much, but in the way mentioned before. They may use prayer to resolve urgent and important matters, but in fact are artificial.

Here is an example to help make this clearer. A priest is very attached to a parish where he has been stationed. He has had many friends there, good food, and excellent living arrangements. Now he is discerning a transfer to another parish. He is very conscious of his ties to his current position, but instead of praying for freedom of heart, he proposes to the Lord how important his commitment is to this city. Wouldn't his continued dedication to pastoral work among this parish of sophisticated adults not be more profitable than beginning some kind of outreach to marginalized youth who have already been exposed to the evils of society? With such a prayer the priest gradually convinces himself that he should remain in his current place. This is a classic example of how a person maintains an attachment and makes something else the problem.

In order to unmask self-love in a true testing of the will, we need to ask the Lord for the grace to be free to leave behind *or* to maintain something that is good in itself, to sustain a project *or* not to sustain it, asking that our only goal be that of surrendering to what God wants. And this is not all. It is even necessary to ask the Lord that he himself be the one to move our wills toward what is good for us and that he give us the grace not to want either one or the other if that desire is not moved by his love and our love for him. By becoming freer, we renounce our own considerations, that is, we opt for what we believe is the best way for walking with the Lord and serving him.

There is still the danger that we could leave this prayer in the abstract, that is, renouncing everything and doing nothing, indulging ourselves in laziness under the pretext of freedom, so that we're bound by nothing and ready for everything, without ever actually taking any step. In this case, self-love would have won again. In order to avoid this trap, spiritual writers advise us to accentuate the connection between will and life. To be sure that we have no ties and are truly free, without any subtle propensity for one thing or another, the spiritual masters counsel us to sincerely give the Lord that to which we could be attached: the gifts, intentions, projects, etc.

And if we offer, the Lord can take. He knows that if it is better for us to have these realities, he will give them to us, or else he will withhold them. Even if he gives these things back to us, we will use them—and live them—in a truly spiritual way, because we will know that they are not ours. We will be able to love through them, rather than being deluded that we are acting in love, while in reality are seeking only ourselves. It is impossible to put oneself into God's hands, to follow the Lord, or to serve love while seeking to assert one's own will.

To be sure that we are truly offering ourselves, the spiritual masters advise us even to ask for the opposite of what we desire. That is, if something is particularly dear to me, I ask the Lord to take it, and, if I am afraid of or dislike something, I begin to ask for the grace to be able to accept that too. The spiritual masters are aware that this is counterintuitive, but it can also be precisely the connection with lived experience, with life, to the field of true testing.

> It is impossible to put oneself into God's hands, to follow the Lord, or to serve love while seeking to assert one's own will.

The true testing of the will is made in relation to the person of Christ, because he is the complete expression and gift of divine love and agape, his life totally handed over to the Father's will. It is precisely in the sacrifice of his will that Christ fully reveals himself as the Son of God, Savior of humanity. In Gethsemani, Christ entrusted his entire being to the will of the Father, thus surrendering himself to the Father's will. He wants what the Father wants, which is more than simply entrusting himself to the will of another. In Gethsemani, Christ's will is expressed precisely in wanting what the Father wants. The Father wants the salvation of the world, that is, that humanity discover itself loved by God, that it see that it is God who takes the first step and places himself into the hands of humanity, considering it worthy of his trust.

For Christ, however, all of this means that he must give himself over into the hands of a sinful generation at odds with God. For Christ in Gethsemani, entrusting his will to the Father means delivering himself into paternal hands, which are the hands of the soldiers who came to arrest him. The sacrifice of Christ's own will saves us, but this salvation is carried out in the concrete circumstances of the passion. It is not simply a nice idea or some religious or moral romanticism.

For us, achieving freedom of will means admitting that not everything we choose to do with our wills is going to be good. Sooner or later we realize that the true good lies outside our own efforts. The highest religious act consists in admitting that we can only think, know, desire, and wish to carry out the good, while in reality not only are we incapable of carrying out the good but, in thinking that we are implementing good, we are often also actually doing evil. We want to do good, but instead do the evil that we do not want to do: "When I want to do what is good, evil lies close at hand" (Rom 7:21).

Only in renouncing our own wills and adhering to the will of him who not only knows the good but is also Goodness itself, possesses good, and therefore does it, do we have any hope that what we are doing might be good. The will, when it refuses to make itself the protagonist, sacrifices itself and becomes the vessel prepared for the will of true Love, who alone is capable of realizing a complete gift of self-surrendered love.

St. Ignatius of Loyola, when suggesting prayers for testing the will, insists on colloquy. What are these colloquies St. Ignatius refers to so frequently, already underlining their importance in the examination of one's way of thinking? One form of prayer is reflection, and Ignatius speaks at times of using reflection as we examine our will. As a great master of prayer, however, he is very aware that when we reflect, think, or ponder in prayer, we can easily find ourselves alone: it is very easy to slip from a relationship with God to being absorbed in religious, devout, or highly spiritual thoughts that are not necessarily authentic prayer. Prayer is a conscious relationship with God.

For Ignatius, colloquy makes explicit the true nature of prayer, which is an opening of ourselves to the Lord, keeping him not only in our thoughts, intentions, and desires, but also questioning, asking, proposing, waiting, welcoming, accepting him.... These are words that express the relational attitude of a person in a true dialogue with another living person.

Colloquies, so important for one's free adherence to Christ, guard the authenticity of one's prayer and spiritual journey, because they are only possible, first, if one feels oneself to be vitally incorporated into the Church so that one has a certain familiarity with the saints; and second, if from within the contemplation of the trinitarian communion and love, one is able to speak to the three divine Persons about what one desires in prayer. If we look at the Ignatian text, these colloquies are often his questions, requests, or intentions that, precisely because they are expressed as a conversation, mature his readiness to welcome what God suggests to him.

In this examination of the will, where there is the greater risk of deception, delusion, or deviation, prayer must be much more authentic. The history of Christian spirituality testifies to the great risk of spiritual errors and illnesses because of an incorrect understanding of the role of the will and its incorrect use in the spiritual life. One can be almost careless in one's language about good intentions and keeping resolutions. The spiritual life is paved with good resolutions, under which masquerades an impure ego. One might even propose to increase one's ascetic practices, fixing one's gaze on an ideal and perfect image one has of oneself, only to become embittered, desolate, and deprived of the fruits of the spiritual life.

We need to ask ourselves if we are truly handing over our wills, unfettered by all ties and attachments to things and projects, desiring them only if God wants them for us. Only in this way shall fulfilling our wills be done in love. In this life, however, doing things in love means going through the passion. The sacrifice of one's own will is an inner act, but it is charged with the paschal sacrifice that is then carried out in the suffering of everyday history. The two dimensions of Christ in Gethsemani return: the Father and the arrest.

Testing One's Way of Loving[4]

The final testing of one's complete surrender to Christ is that of humility, or of love. Here one is dealing with how much one's fundamental attitude is truly a radical recognition of the Other or how much resistance still remains. St. Ignatius structured this testing on three levels. The first level helps us to see if God is truly first in our hearts, if anyone or anything is competing with the Creator. It is a little like the scene of Eden at the moment of the world's creation. Human beings, placed in creation and having a lively and strong relationship with the Creator, are ordered by God not to eat from a certain tree. As long as they do not eat of that tree, which is the voice of their desire, then the first voice in their hearts is that of God and nothing else can present itself as an alternative to him. The spiritual masters say that even life itself cannot be in competition with God. God is first. God is life, and we, precisely because we are redeemed by God, have an experiential knowledge of life and are alive thanks only to him. Without God there is no life. This is why there is nothing, no matter how fascinating and brilliant, that can convince us even for an instant that there is any life outside of love for God.

This first level of the testing of my love, therefore, manifests my religious foundation, that is, the awareness and affirmation of God, the prostrating of myself before God, admitting that he is the first, the source, and that I am only a creature. In this way, my humility is tested; that is, I see if I have already experienced the salvation of God to such a degree that I am certain that I can do nothing of myself, and that it is only in finding my epicenter in God that I can be authentically fulfilled. Humility—in the sense of having a definitive and absolute support not in myself but *in* the Other and *with* the Other—is love. This attitude of humility, however, can only exist if I know myself to be loved by God, if love is already an experiential awareness in me, a certainty. Therefore, the spiritual masters suggest a further step.

> It is only in finding my epicenter in God that I can be authentically fulfilled.

After determining that we are not deceiving ourselves, but are voluntarily pronouncing our adherence to Christ and our unconditioned belief in him, then we can look even more carefully at our love. This second moment in the testing of our love makes us see if the Lord is so precious to us that there is nothing we can do, desire, or will except to be with him and to do what he wants. It is an attitude wherein our entire focus is on the Other, not daring to desire either long or short lives for ourselves, sickness or health, etc. Even if either choice would lead to our salvation, we do not choose for ourselves. Attention is thus moved toward the Lord. The Lord is everything for us, and we do not want to lose anything of him. Our only desire is an ever more complete focus on him, to consider him ever more completely. Thus the most common things concerning our lives, and choices about even pleasurable, useful, and convenient things, no longer attract us because it is only the Lord that we find attractive, the Lord and what he wants for our lives, since only the Lord knows and prepares our life journeys. At this point, not only are we unwilling to break away from God, attracted by other things that seem more precious than God, but love pushes us toward such intimacy with the Lord that we do not want to lose even the smallest occasion to attend to him.

The third moment of the testing of love is supreme and total. One has experientially known the Lord as the paschal Messiah—not just the omnipotent God, a miracle-working Messiah, a prophet powerful in words, or a Master wise in doctrine, but the paschal Lord. The awareness between the Lord and the believer is so intimate and total that the believer asks for the grace to be able to participate with him in disgrace, in being denied like him, and in being considered mad. If the believer lived an intense spiritual life and enjoyed success, health, and acceptance among others and, notwithstanding all this, asked the Lord for the grace to suffer humiliation

with him, this would be absolutely crazy. Someone could
make such a request only if that person were not in his or
her right mind. Or else, someone who had been touched
by God's love and could no longer forget the features of
his Face; someone who knows what is true and what is
false, what is illusion and what is reality, even with regard
to God. Only someone could ask for this who understands
that Christianity is not a *discourse* about Christ, about
values, and about the Gospel, but is God's crazy love for
humanity and humanity's love for God in return. It is so
crazy a love that no worldly logic can uphold it, because it
can only be understood by an intelligence of agape.

The door to the knowledge of God is an experiential
awareness of this love that gives itself away, a love characterized by a truly personal encounter with God. The
person of God is so real for us that we feel impelled only
by love. For no other reason—neither convenience nor
ethical imperatives—but out of love alone do we want to
spend our lives following the Lord, together with him,
going through what he went through. Being this close to
Christ, everything that happened to him also happens to
whomever loves him.

This is not "imitating" Christ in a formal way. Love
makes us similar to the one loved and urges us to take
the steps he has taken, to make the gestures he has made,
and to think as he thinks. If we can ask for the grace to
be this close to Christ, to be so radically rooted in him as
to undergo the most concrete aspects of his paschal love,
then we practically declare that our lives have a sole
value: being consumed for love together with the life of
Christ. Those who dare to ask for this grace have
acquired that paschal attitude that only the Holy Spirit

can communicate and imprint on the human heart. They are therefore not bound by ideologies, moralism, or psychologism. They are authentically religious persons.

The fundamental characteristic of this love is humility. It is achieved by suffering many humiliations in love and because of love. The greatest humiliation along the path of following the Lord, however, is sin. Only in the encounter with the Face of love can Christians live this humiliation in the passage to humility. Once having achieved such humility, Christians are capable of carrying out their ministry or vocation precisely because they are no longer preoccupied with themselves. They can therefore be completely consigned and dedicated to what God asks of them. If they suffer disgrace, provocation, or even persecution, they do not respond to the insults, do not argue with those who contradict and fight with them.

This testing of love reveals also a Christian's maturity in reference to belonging to the Church, in that belonging to Christ means belonging to his Church. The three levels of testing correspond to different levels of a maturity of belonging. We can be in the Church without consciously accepting a personal experience of God's salvation, but only by the simple fact that our Baptism has incorporated us into the Church. We live what the Church lives in her apostolic tradition, accepting the commandments and precepts as helps that sustains us in our journey toward the Lord. In this case, the precepts are a gift on the part of the ecclesial community to these Christians.

Then, there are those who live very close relationships with Christ, have consciously accepted his love, and have handed themselves over to him; those who are further away from Christians at this level of belonging, seeing the example of these more mature Christians, feel the inspiration to live like them, trying to imitate their ways of thinking and acting. In this case, both the Holy Spirit and the testimony of the baptized are gifts that permeate the Church. Clearly, in a time of plurality such as our own, those who live their ecclesial belonging in a somewhat weak manner are continually tempted to surrender their faithfulness because their experiential knowledge of the Lord is weak. For example, the person who participates in the Sunday Eucharist only because it is a law of the Church will find the commitment difficult to sustain in a world where there are a thousand other possible activities. A time will no doubt come when he or she will feel less motivated to go to Mass on Sunday.

Instead, those who have personal awareness of the salvation of Christ and who live with him such strong relationships that they even ask for the grace to participate in his destiny and to be made similar to him in the most trying aspects of his passion—these people cannot wait to be with Christ and their brothers and sisters at the Sunday Eucharist. It is not the law but love that urges them to be with Christ, whom they love and who loves them. For these people, then, the law almost does not exist because they reason and feel from within the meaning of the law. For those who are at the first level, the law easily becomes a constriction, a prohibition, an obstacle to something else. For mature Christians, the law sustains them in moments of weakness, in moments when their relationships with Christ are difficult and they are going through spiritual dryness. Moreover, whoever lives a strong relationship with Christ also perceives the Church—in her entire dramatic dimension—in the way she leads to purification.

Prayer for Full Surrender to Christ[5]

We go about these testings of our ways of thinking, willing, and loving in prayer, not as the intellectual pursuit of some high ideal. This prayer is based on the contemplation of Christ's life and, above all, the paschal mystery. Mature Christians are often bent over Sacred Scripture, pondering especially the pages of the Lord's passion, death, and resurrection. They contemplate the paschal mystery and taste Christ's love in order to grasp what he feels, which is the way God feels toward humanity. The contemplation of Scripture is a prayer to the Holy Spirit, that he might always more fully involve us in and disclose to us the mystery of Christ, that he might unite us completely to Christ. It is, therefore, a prayer of supplication, of asking. It is a prayer of vows and commitments in which, on the basis of humility, we dare to ask for the grace of intimacy with Christ.

It is helpful to examine ourselves as a part of the method of prayer presented in Part I of this volume. When this examination is done repeatedly, it is useful to think over these examinations throughout the day, to contemplate many times the Face and gestures of Christ, hearing his words again. When I must make an important decision, I return frequently to the option that is closest to my desire. I frequently return to the path I want to take and allow my thoughts to be interrupted often by the prayer for full adherence to Christ, along with a contemplation of Christ's life, my intense and sincere petitions, and my commitment in spirit before him. The days thus pass in a continual correspondence between prayer for Christ's mentality, freedom, and love, and my own thoughts, projects, and preoccupations. My reasoning and thoughts enter into a constant relationship with Christ, an ever-deeper relationship characterized by a more authentic and purified love.

This prayer for full adherence and surrender also becomes a type of "filter" for our thoughts, intentions, and projects. The spiritual Fathers advise us to take a thought, linger over it, and, while we are thinking about it, to try to enter with Christ into the paschal triduum, to read the passion narratives. If this thought helps us remain united to Christ, as if stitched to him, while we run with him along the paschal path, then it could be a thought inspired by the Holy Spirit. If, instead, this thought weakens, becomes frightened, or disappears, it is evidently vain, empty, or inspired by our disguised self-love. This is why it is very useful, at the end of the day or a time of prayer, to write down some key points of what happened during prayer.

The Attitude of Discernment[6]

Those who courageously wage a spiritual struggle against all the illusions and traps that the tempter lays for them frequently acquire a paschal mentality through prayer, coming to a relative freedom of will, and acquiring a purification of their minds, feelings, and wills. They achieve an integration of their hearts that makes it possible to think spiritually, feel spiritually, will spiritually, and act spiritually. The journey to this goal is studded with testings that are practically a continuous prayer and that definitively and firmly engrave the figure of Christ on our hearts in order to make us grow to full maturity. The Holy Spirit conforms the human heart to Christ, for it was through his power that the Word was made flesh in Mary, and the Holy Spirit makes us truly think more and more with Christ and like Christ; we begin to discover the gift of feeling Christ's sentiments within our hearts and to desire what Christ desires. In short, as Christians we begin to reason, feel, and will as children of God; a lifestyle of children in the Son begins to shine through each day. This lifestyle is the assurance that we now have the ability to discern, to put spirits to the test, to discover true inspirations of the Holy Spirit and to follow them. We begin to know "what is of Babylon and what is of Jerusalem." We become persons who can discover treasures of the faith even in the depths of the netherworld and see mourning in the greatest of celebrations.

Persons who have matured to this level no longer need to follow precise methods of discernment, because they already have the attitude that allows them to read and discern what happens to them and what is presented to their minds. They have reached that state of humility that allows God to reveal himself, that attitude of humble love that disposes them in such a way as to be able to welcome the revelation of the Holy Spirit. God gives himself to the humble and opposes the proud (cf. 1 Pt 5:5). St. Ignatius himself, for example, with all his mastery of the rules and techniques of discernment, over time no longer discerned according to his own rules, because he no longer needed to. In the beginning, he posed many questions and made many attempts to discover God's will. In the end, we find him much more peaceful and surprisingly firm, because the degree of purification he had reached allowed him to contemplate God.

The ancients frequently spoke of the purification of the mind, that is, one's ways of thinking and feeling. Certainly the reason is obvious: to achieve an integration of all the cognitive capacities in the heart, to come as close as one possibly can to a pure heart. A pure heart is a heart that is not torn or darkened by contradictory thoughts that fight among themselves or by conflicting passions that lead one astray. In a pure heart all the dimensions of one's existence that freely adhere to Christ are harmonized.

However, the pure heart is not an empty heart, a clean slate, but a heart so full of a passionate love for Christ that it asks for the grace to conform to him, that Christ might have first place in one's thoughts, feelings, and desires. In reality, Baptism is such an intervention in a person's being, as is the sacrament of Reconciliation, which enables the person to live his or her Baptism in all its strength and richness. This intervention of the grace of the Holy Spirit brings with it also a change in one's "gnoseology," the art of spiritual perception. We are not familiar with this thought today, but the ancients used it often, as do the great modern spiritual authors. A purified heart means a new spiritual perception. We intuit clearly what draws us to Christ and what draws us away from him, what is from Christ and what is not, because we have reached such a degree of inner freedom that everything that happens to us does not provoke us to reaction, but fixes our eyes only on the Lord. We are no longer harmed by self-preoccupation.

The Object of Discernment[7]

In our lives, we make decisions and choices about many things. Some choices are definitive, for example, marriage, the priesthood, and religious vows. These choices, because of their irrevocable nature, are delicate aspects of our spiritual journeys. Here the spiritual struggle will certainly be more intense, because the enemy will do everything possible to keep us from fulfilling God's will and to spur us to choose our own wills instead. But if one's life vocation is already determined, then one's choices have to do with an improvement in one's state of life—that is, how to adhere more completely to Christ in the life one has chosen.

It can happen—and in fact often does—that one realizes with relative clarity that one has made a mistake in the choice of one's state of life. One then vigorously embraces the choice one has made with a penitent attitude, that is, with a state of purifying humility based only on the Lord's mercy. This humility facilitates the stripping of the person's heart of his or her own desires and making choices each day so that the person's heart can be further exposed to God's love, in order that this love might pass through the person and penetrate his or her history and surroundings, reaching those nearest the person.

All the important choices that arise in life that in some way radically touch our personal spiritual journeys—as well as the choices we have already made—enter into this discernment. Examples of such choices can be whether to build a house, what job to take, whether to change jobs or one's place of work, whether to move to another area, and so on. These decisions certainly should not be taken lightly because through them it is possible to begin to break away from one's surrender to Christ and slowly to find oneself to be the protagonist of one's life, isolated, and prey to self-affirming powers that empty and feed on one, becoming truly a force that destroys the journey one has made thus far.

Discernment for a greater surrender to Christ also touches personal relationships, friendships, the places we visit, and the things that we see, listen to, or read. Even choices concerning daily expenditures—what we buy, the money we spend—where we choose to go to have fun and relax, the way we dress and present ourselves, are not innocuous. All these choices spring from an overall vision, but the continuity of choices also affects these visions or orientations. If we do not have a spiritual approach to handling these small but important daily realities, we either overlook them or handle them in a moralistic perspective according to the rule of, "What am I allowed to do? What is forbidden? How far can I go?" Slowly, these criteria eat away at the overall structure of the lives we think we have. How often we meet people who regret the steps they have been deceived into taking because they were involved with the wrong people, or allowed themselves to be influenced at inopportune moments, or chose the wrong workplaces, or bet their lives on whims or ideas that turned out to be worthless. They struggled and fought for things that seemed fundamental and worthy of the sacrifice of energy and time, but which were ultimately insignificant details, small and petty matters.

The prayer for discernment also concerns the ability to read the signs of the times. To discern what is happening means being capable of seeing spiritual meanings under the dross of publicity, beneath the glitter in culture, information, and the mass media; of unmasking the exaggeration of various spheres of power that magnify events according to their own spins; and above all of being capable of seeing the connections between events and the history of salvation that continues to play itself out. Discernment is choosing whether to read history and interpret events in the light of salvation history, or to accept, more or less consciously, the interpretation of others.

In both cases it is a matter of a choice that, added to the other choices one makes, becomes a horizon. That horizon can be an actual structure of thought that is

> Discernment is choosing whether to read history and interpret events in the light of salvation history, or to accept the interpretation of others.

an iron-clad armor imprisoning the spirit, suffocating the heart, killing faith, and making one rigid, bitter, narrow-minded, and myopic. Or it can lead one, through the art of continuous discernment, to broad horizons, to a dynamic, dialogical, religious approach that is in continuous surrender to the Christ of the eternal pasch.

CHAPTER 8

Practicing Discernment[1]

THE HUMAN PERSON IS A LIVING BEING, capable of entering into dialogue with God and the world. The spiritual journey is made on the path of wisdom. We have too often been tempted to schematize people, reducing them to theories and analyses in order to understand them exhaustively, to explain their reactions, their ways of being, and with these explanations, to condition them.

The history of spirituality indicates the catastrophic implications that this has for the human soul, the life of faith, and, therefore, for the person's salvation. History is full of conceptualizations of the human person. We have often found ourselves enslaved by theories.

This is why it is necessary to point out once again that one shouldn't seek, even in the prayer of discernment, a technique to apply or a recipe to follow. A person's journey cannot be defined by clean, precise, or automatic stages of spiritual growth, as discernment itself shows, precisely because it is a journey of dialogue sealed between the person and Christ, in the Church, within a communal memory, tradition, and exclusively by the light of the Holy Spirit.

It is clear that the radical reconciliation brought about through the encounter with the Face of a merciful God, as described in the first part of this volume, is not an annual occurrence, but it is nevertheless true that the person will still have many battles with sin to fight. In the same way, the struggle against the enemy's deceptions is not a once-and-for-all event through which we definitively learn the enemy's tactics and can live peacefully forevermore. Rather it is a struggle that accompanies us our entire lives. Even more, the further we go on this path, the more arduous it becomes and the more difficult the struggle.

The prayer thanks to which we achieve greater surrender to Christ humiliated, denied, and abandoned in the passion is not made once and for all, after which it automatically becomes the Christian's *forma mentis* [mind set]. Rather, it is a continuous journey that has strong movements, but which, at its nucleus, is a constant memory of God preserved through daily prayer. We need to exercise discernment in order gradually to reach, with an experiential wisdom, that state of a continuous attitude of discernment.

In discerning about a choice one needs to make, when one is not yet penetrated by Christ's way of thinking, willing, and loving, spiritual tradition suggests using a method. When discernment becomes second nature, one will no longer need a method. Until then, however, a method for making a discernment is useful. Discernment in this sense is a spiritual exercise by which one follows the steps laid out in the spiritual tradition for reaching spiritual clarity regarding a choice one needs to make so as to be certain one is following God's inspiration.

Three "Times" of Discernment

The first "time" in which I can make a good choice—that is, can see reality with God's eyes—is when my adherence to Christ, my intimate friendship with him, has endured for a long time. I feel intensely attracted by the Lord and by his love. The attraction is strong; the memory of Christ is almost constant, welling up within my heart. While experiencing this attraction to Christ, I find that this choice lies along the path to Christ and is totally enveloped in my integral surrender to the paschal Christ.

With a strong sense of Christ's love, there is not even a possibility of doubting that this is what will lead me on a radical *sequela Christi*. I am, however, free; I feel a strong love for the Lord and clearly see that the reality of the choice belongs to the sphere of this love. I do not perceive it as an imposed duty nor feel an urgency or pressure that produces haste and attachments, as when I am possessed by an intuition or a thought. Rather, I sense a radical orientation toward the real, true Christ, and in this orientation the choice presents itself as an integral part, as an element of my complete surrender to Christ. My interior freedom, a real fruit of the Holy Spirit, guarantees that this is not a disguised attachment. It is a spiritual freedom where Christ is the priority. Everything is ordered rightly, and I have no doubts or anxiety, which are normally the signs of obstinacy and disordered attachment because I am afraid to lose what is dear to me.

This is called a first-time experience, and we can calmly choose that which is within this attraction to Christ.

The second "time" in which I can make a good choice is a time of spiritual memory that is strengthened by the consolations and desolations I have experienced in my prayer about the choice to be made. Since I have already seen that inspirations that bring me to be at peace in the love of my Savior are inspired by the Holy Spirit, I slowly come to a greater clarity on which states of being are most opened to the Holy Spirit and which, instead, to the discord and distress provoked by the tempter. On the basis of this clarity I choose what will bring me to a greater surrender to Christ, to a more complete nearness and openness to the Lord.

This means, therefore, I need to care for my spiritual memory, making good use of the examinations in my times of prayer that bring to light what happens in my soul as I reflect and pray about the choice to be made. With time I recognize what helps my surrender to Christ and what, instead, disrupts it. When this memory is well-strengthened and clarified, when I can immediately recognize where my inner movements come from and where they lead, it is the opportune moment to make my choice. At this time of inner clarity, there is little possibility of being duped into following the movements prompted by the enemy, since I know from experience where they lead.

In this way I choose the reality that is found within moments of spiritual consolation.

The third "time" in which to make a choice is in moments of tranquility, when my soul is not upset by the various temptations that stir it and make it scatter here and there; they are moments of spiritual serenity and inner tranquility characterized by a firm, radical orientation to Christ. I have a strong experience of my encounter with Christ and know how it has transformed me with a real and palpable love of God. This love remains so unmistakable and strong that now I see the Lord as my only goal in life. The Lord is the only reason for my life, and I want nothing other than to remain with him, to do his will, and to serve him in every way I can in order to reach the eternal, complete encounter with the One whom I have anticipated. The soul's tranquility comes from an ordered heart.

This state of being is in some way similar to that of the first time for making a decision, only here I do not feel an explicit and immediate innate attraction regarding what must be chosen. Because of the tranquility of my emotions and reason, however, I can use my reason in a spiritual way, discovering the decisions to take to reach my proper fulfillment in God's love.

In this third time, St. Ignatius suggests two ways to make a choice.

The first way

- You begin to pray, bringing the purpose of your life into focus. You renew your belonging entirely to Christ. Your heart is moved by gratitude and, in an attitude of recognition and respect, you renew your surrender to the great sense of life, which is the Lord, and entrust yourself to him so that he might act in you and through you in history.

- You then briefly present the alternatives for the choice at hand and check to make sure you are interiorly free regarding them.

- You ask the Holy Spirit to keep you free from passionate attachments and try to determine the level of your spiritual indifference. Ignatius says one is to become like the needle of a scale. Your "needle" moves only after reasoning through what is best for your more complete surrender to Christ and for his glory in the world. It is therefore necessary to go through the prayer of discernment, asking the Lord to move your will toward what will be best for your salvation and for a more complete openness to Christ's love.

- At the end of these extremely important preparatory prayers, you begin to ponder, reflecting with your intellect on the choice to be made. Begin by considering what would happen if you decided for the matter in question. List in a column the advantages that deciding for this choice has for your adherence to Christ and his presence in the world.

- Then consider and list in a second column all the disadvantages it will mean for your surrender to Christ and for the salvation of the world.

- Afterward, do the same as if you were deciding against the matter in question, listing in separate columns the advantages and disadvantages in regard to your intimate adherence to Christ and the salvation of the world.

- At the end, you have four columns of advantages and disadvantages. Call upon the Holy Spirit and renew the sense of the larger meaning of your life before the Lord. As you read and ponder over the advantages and disadvantages, you see what your reason tends toward and, on the basis of this greater impetus of your reason, you choose.

St. Ignatius was aware of the risk of an exaggerated dependence on a method, endowing it with a magical power, which would open the door to self-assertion. So he prescribes offering the choice one has made to the Lord with a prayer in which one asks the Lord to accept and confirm it if it is his will and if he wants it. Asking for confirmation, which should be done with care and sincerity, is of great importance. It brings one back to one's vocation. A Christian's choices, if they are true, are always a response to a call, a surrender to the Lord's will, a love that responds to love. It is impossible to force God to accept the choices we make, thinking that he must be pleased with them.

Within a rationalistic culture we could think that this way of discernment is the most trustworthy, because it uses reason and not an awareness of our feelings in spiritual consolation. But if we recall what was said previously about the possibility of our thoughts being influenced by passion, we see that this method of making a choice is probably one of the most risky. In fact, our passions and attachments can be camouflaged by reason's apparent objectivity. It's very helpful, if one uses this method of making a decision, to submit the process and one's motivations to a spiritual person used to guiding discernments who can see if the advantages one noted have only to do with the Lord, one's surrender to him, and the world's salvation, or if in reality, within the list of advantages and disadvantages, a disguised self-love and disordered attachments are hiding.

The second way

- In this second way, you immerse yourself in prayer, recalling God's love. At the beginning of the prayer, you relive the love that comes only from God and reaches you as truly experienced salvation, a salvation that gives you the capacity to love with a love that has its only source in Christ's love for you. You become aware that God's love is first and your love is a response. Love is the great meaning of your life, not as your own merit or doing, but as a gift received and a collaboration in God's grace, in his love. In this way, the desire you feel toward the matter under consideration is also moved solely by love for Christ, as a response to his love.

- You then imagine a person you have never met, for whom you desire every good, every perfection, and a more complete surrender to Christ for his or her salvation. In prayer, in dialogue with the Lord, you advise this person as to what he or she should choose and what he or she should do. Then you follow the advice you have given.

- Continuing in an attitude of authentic prayer, imagine yourself at the hour of your death, when you no longer have the possibility of turning back, changing, trying again, or even of cheating. Then in prayer before the Lord try to see how you would have wanted to act regarding the choice under consideration. That is how you decide now. The great spiritual masters of Christian tradition highly esteemed this exercise of remembering one's death.

No doubt this exercise leads to sobriety, to the essentials, and it reduces the capacity for deception and pretense.

• Remaining in this dialogue of prayer, imagine yourself before God as you would want to be at the hour of judgment regarding the matter you are about to decide. As you wished you would have done, standing at your judgment before the Lord, Judge of history, decide now in the choice you are about to make.

• You conclude your prayer by making, through these three steps, your choice, and then presenting yourself before the Lord, in all humility, asking him to accept your decision if it is pleasing to him, because he knows if it is truly good for you. The Lord's confirmation will show you that you are choosing the right thing, that you are responding to his will.

Just as in the first way there is a strong risk of reasoning with passion, so in the second way it is necessary to be attentive to the psychological structure of the person making the decision, that is, to the entirety of his or her personality and history, because vulnerabilities, habits, vices, fears, or emotional wounds from what was lived in the past can greatly influence the imagination. That is why one's choice here should now be tested by ascertaining in prayer how radical one's openness is and to what extent Christ and love for him are one's supreme goal. How strong are these spiritual memories in one's imagination? Today's culture, profoundly marked by sensual and violent images, certainly conditions our imaginations. Without purifying the imagination it can be used only with difficulty in prayer, especially in prayer for the discernment of important choices.

Accompanied by a spiritual guide, the first two times are the privileged moments for making choices in the tradition of the Church. This third time, with its two ways, is certainly more exposed to possible delusions, as pointed out. Even in this time, it is therefore important to have the presence of a spiritual guide. One makes choices through discernment and spiritual struggle, not as an individual, but rather as an integral part of a living and wise organism: the Church. That is why we should submit our choices to persons of great spiritual authority, asking for spiritual advice, which is a permanent praxis of the ecclesial tradition.

Two related questions should be noted with regard to this. One is about spiritual authority. Those who have spiritual authority do not possess it *ex officio*, but as a charism in the ministry of spiritual accompaniment, of spiritual fatherhood or motherhood, as persons who are truly initiated in the life and spiritual wisdom of the Church's tradition. They are persons in whom the saints of tradition breathe, think, feel, and reflect. They are persons with a practical sense and an innate understanding of human psychology, who know and can penetrate the subtle interweaving between the psychological and the spiritual, between the cultural and the theological. They are masters of the spiritual struggle.

It is difficult in our day to find true experts of life in the Holy Spirit. Spiritual guides are often substituted with those who are competent in the human sciences, areas that are very useful, yet always auxiliary. Our time is characterized by immanence, in which people are locked within psychosomatic or socio-cultural structures, as if there were no serious belief in the existence of the spirit. We study the body, we study the psyche, but we do not study the spirit with the same seriousness. As a consequence we do not consider the spirit as an autonomous reality that has it own dynamics, its own knowledge, and its own implications. Often we project the psychic or intellectual sphere onto the world of the spirit. The search for a person who is an expert in the human spirit and life in the Holy Spirit is thus more difficult today.

The second question regards the persons seeking advice. Often, since they are uninitiated in a sapiential life, they take the advice they receive as teaching, and their tendency is to carry out what their directors told them, with the risk that they exchange roles with the directors. One goes to a spiritual director not to lose one's personality or to abandon one's own responsibility, but for the certainty that the truth is love and therefore it is in communion that one knows oneself. The authentic dimension of ecclesiality is certainly the path of spiritual awareness, and it has always been the practice of our Christian tradition that we share the spiritual struggle, our uncertainties, decisions, and even responsibilities.

Since our age is marked by an accentuated individualism and self-validation, it is easy to have a dialectical attitude when going to a spiritual director. Instead, one should go with an attitude of humility, which tradition emphasizes above all as docility, that is, allowing things to be said to one. This means being attentive to what the director says, beginning to dialogue with the Lord in prayer regarding these words, encountering and conversing with this thought in order to let it become fruitful in our life.

CHAPTER 9

Vocation[1]

ONE OF THE OBJECTS OF DISCERNMENT in this second phase is the choice of a state of life, or rather, the response to one's vocation. Regarding this it is important to underline some indispensable points for a healthy choice of vocation.

— The Christian vocation is a response to the call to life with which God creates every person. The Holy Spirit participates in the Father's love for humanity. God cannot want for anything apart from himself because he is everything, totality. Since God is love, his will is love. God the Father has just one desire for the entire human race: that it discover itself as loved by him, that we members of the human race allow ourselves to be penetrated by his love and thus complete creation's becoming according to the Father's design, passing from darkness to light, from sin to salvation, from death to resurrection.

The Christian vocation is the means through which we open ourselves most fully to the love that God the Father has given to us in creation. He wants to penetrate us completely with this love until it reaches the world outside us. The Christian vocation is the call to a progressive penetration by the Holy Spirit, which pours the Father's love into our hearts (cf. Rom 5:5). It is a path to conquering all the resistance that sin triggers in us, making us rebel against love and locking us up in selfishness.

Now, it is obvious that every person has a path in life through which to open himself or herself more radically to love, realizing the life and grace of Baptism and putting into more effective action the grace of witnessing conferred in Confirmation. We cannot all walk the same path. Some people, if they remain single, will be more easily conquered by temptations or selfishness. Other people in the single state will be able to open themselves more to love and more easily burn away their selfishness to the very core. We could say this about vocations in the sense of states of life, as well as about vocations, professions, or careers.

To search for our own vocations means seeking how to respond to God's will so that we will be penetrated with his love, that we will be made sons and daughters of the Holy Spirit, and that we live today as God's children. According to the Christian vision, vocation aims at the resurrection of our bodies, at the resurrection of our persons, because a vocation is fulfilled by dying to selfishness, by sacrificing our own wills, and by opening ourselves to the love of God the Father infused in us daily by the Holy Spirit. Everything that is imbued with the Father's love is snatched away from death for the resurrection, because the Father's love remains for all eternity.

Love, as has been said, is carried out in a paschal way. This means that the Christian vocation is a path along which we are consumed in a sacrifice of love, because we do not withhold ourselves but, urged on by love, offer ourselves up. Whoever loves is consumed, just as a seed that falls to the earth disappears in order to germinate new life. The Christian vocation is radically and essentially imprinted with the paschal journey, where there are no heroes who throw themselves into sacrifices of their own choosing, but only disciples of Christ who walk in Christ's footsteps, in conformity to him, illuminated and sustained by the Holy Spirit.

— If it is God who calls me, then it is evident that I must encounter him. It is much easier to find my vocation and to feel it as something that comes from within me if I first experience God's love in a profound and radical reconciliation with him. If I have an authentic experience of being saved by the Lord, I will be much more capable of understanding that it is the Lord who calls and I who respond. This experience will save me from the classic trap in choosing a vocation to try to buy God's love, to appear better, make reparation, get a fresh start, improve myself, redeem myself, etc.

> Those who have experienced salvation, who have been truly touched by love, will not fall into the mistake of planning their lives on their own, but will seek to put themselves at God's disposition.

Those who have experienced salvation, who have been truly touched by love, will not fall into the mistake of planning their lives on their own, but will seek to put themselves at God's disposition, making themselves available. They will propose to God the possibilities with detachment and with free hearts, capable of seeing which of these proposals are the Lord's will. Vocation, therefore, is a dialogical question fulfilled in a sealed relationship between God and the individual within the Church. Vocation is not a plan one makes for one's life, isolated from the community.

— An initial vocational discernment begins with gathering the different voices that can enlighten a person in this search: personal talents, character strengths and weaknesses, cultural conditioning, social placement, education, friendships, persons who have had a strong influence on him or her, the Church that calls according to the needs of the time, the needs and sufferings of Christians in different parts of the world, the Gospel that suffers violence. Also one ponders the situation in which one finds oneself without seeking, planning, or desiring it—this strong context that is a type of crossroads of the great historical coordinates that demand a total response from those who are able to interpret the importance of events. One considers all these realities and slowly catches sight of a type of harmony, as if in a large mosaic one were beginning to understand the significance of each individual piece.

— Before coming to an actual decision regarding my vocation, it is important that I spend some time walking in the direction suggested by this symphony of voices. I should also use my imagination, trying to see myself in the state of life being suggested, beside that partner, in a family for example, or in a mission or convent.... I should try to activate all my cognitive abilities in times of prayer in which I imagine myself in the vocation to which I perceive that the Voice, uniting all the diverse voices, is calling me.

— Step by step as the time of the decision draws closer, when one perceives the moment is ripe, one needs to begin working on one's inner freedom. Here, I want to point out particularly two difficulties for young people in today's world. The majority of people develop slowly in their interior freedom. What is more, there is a tendency in people to focus on the ideal, and, as a consequence, they never perceive themselves as having reached the necessary maturity.

It's not that they have a simple fear of definitive commitments, either. Rather, they want to be sure that the lives they choose will bring them satisfaction and affective, emotional pleasure without which they believe they will be unfulfilled and dispossessed. They therefore remain in a prolonged state of emotional dependency, just like the phenomenon of adult children who are still not autonomous from their parents. In order to reach the state wherein we can choose our vocations, however, it is necessary to go through a process of liberation in which we offer everything to the Lord: all our talents, everything we have, everything we are, even the plans we want to follow, and, therefore, even our vocations. Such freedom is obviously the fruit of the Holy Spirit and our collaboration with grace, so it can only happen within the context of prayer. We pray in a very concrete way, in a sincere dialogue, offering the Lord all our gifts, thoughts, and plans. This can also be a painful process, because we are breaking away from our disordered, passionate attachments. This prayer for freedom needs to be repeated many times.

— It is necessary that those who try to imagine themselves on the path they are about to choose be assisted and truly accompanied by the Christ of the paschal triduum. The famous prayers for testing the authenticity of prayer, and therefore the authenticity of one's surrender to Christ, should be part of the process. In prayer, one begins to see the real connection between one's possible vocation and the mystery of Christ's passion and resurrection. Any Christian vocation, if it is to achieve fulfillment in the Lord, must go through the paschal mystery. Or rather, since our vocations and ministries are already fulfilled in Christ—since in him all promises are *already* fulfilled (cf. 2 Cor 1:20)— our personal histories and vocations must be lived according to Christ's way, precisely because he lives in us (cf. Gal 2:20).

> Our personal histories and vocations must be lived according to Christ's way, precisely because he lives in us.

For this reason alone every Christian vocation, in its authenticity, becomes a revelation of Christ and his love for humanity. We must be careful not to seek to classify the value of a vocation morally or according to voluntaristic criteria because, sooner or later, this will break down. In prayer, we simply need to see realistically in each vocation the suffering, failures, defeats, and sorrows of the paschal path. In this adhesion to Christ is their full value. We must perceive these aspects in union with what Christ endured and understand that this is inseparable from the power of the resurrection (cf. Phil 3:10).

— It is good to make a discernment on days of retreat, away from the pressures and distractions of everyday life, in solitude and prayer. Obviously, in this sense discernment is a spiritual exercise. We spend time in prayer in order then to reach the moment of decision according to the circumstances and ways already described.

— Because of the fragile and restless structure of the interior life typical of today's younger generations, it is better that the choice made not be immediately definitive, at least not until the person is seen to be truly mature, not swayed by willfulness and euphoria. Thus it is helpful to accompany the person in a tentative choice, where in dialogue with the Lord a type of covenant is made, and the person lives for a few months or a year as if he or she has assumed this choice. The person then asks that if the Lord accepts the choice, he send the grace of a confirmation; otherwise, that he send signs allowing the person to recognize clearly that he or she is going in the wrong direction. It is clear that the signs of approval and disapproval must be interpreted in spiritual terms and one must use the criteria of the movements of the Holy Spirit and the enemy as earlier described, and not simply an emotional state, created by the satisfaction one feels about what is pleasant.

CHAPTER 10

Communal Discernment[1]

CHRISTIAN COMMUNITIES, IN THIS second stage of discernment, often make discernments about pastoral choices, ministry, or apostolic priorities (to open or close a community in a particular place, to take on one pastoral task or leave another, etc.). For this reason we return to the topic of communal discernment, in which the entire community participates in the choices that are made. In the proper sense of the term, communal discernment does not mean arriving at a decision by considering the sum of the individuals' discernments, but that the community recognizes itself as a living organism, that the persons who make it up create a community of hearts such that the Holy Spirit is able to reveal himself, and that they will see his revelation in this communion of persons, a unity of understanding.

Communal discernment is founded on the love in which the community lives. Fraternal charity is the door to awareness. Love is the cognitive principle; therefore, if members of a community truly live in love, and not just *think* they do, they are in a privileged place for knowing spiritual realities and for creativity. Intuitions and our creative and inventive capacities develop profitably only through love. The community can be much more certain of being on track with God's will—intuited, known, responded to, and discerned as a group—precisely because of the members' love for one another. Communal discernment then isn't a simple debate about a topic or a guided or shared reflection. Communal discernment is not a democratic process or voting.

The Premises of Communal Discernment

For discernment to be carried out in the true sense, there are certain premises that are necessary:

1. The members of the community should all be at a stage of the spiritual life characterized by a radical *sequela Christi*, having reflected deeply on their experience of the paschal Christ. The community members should therefore live and think within the paschal logic and be impelled by an authentic love for Christ, who should be first in their hearts. If members are still stuck in the movements of the soul typical of the first stage of discernment—that is, if they are still on the way toward an authentic experience of Christ in reconciliation—it is obvious that discernment will not happen. In this case, the same reality will appear beautiful to some and ugly to others, like Moses' waters that were clean for the Hebrews and dirty for the Egyptians. Some community members will already think as friends of the cross of Christ, and others, even if they declare to speak in an absolutely spiritual way, will have a way of thinking that sees Christ's cross as foolishness. For some it is evident, even in an experiential way and with firm faith, that each project's path must pass through the paschal triduum.

Others could radically refuse it. They might accept it in words like the others, but in reality they reason as if the project should be carried out avoiding the paschal triduum.

2. The members of the community should have an ecclesial maturity, a theological awareness of the Church that is freed from sociological and psychological determinism, so that they might have a free understanding of authority and a free attitude when faced with it. Obedience is a reality that discloses itself only within faith, in the measure in which we believe that the salvific will of God the Father is mediated and is communicated to each person through the principle of incarnation, since the heart of our faith is the Incarnation.

3. The members should be, at least in principle, ready to enter into prayer in order to free themselves from their own points of view, from their own arguments, and their own desires.

4. It takes human maturity to know how to speak in a detached, placid, and concise manner. It takes maturity to know how to listen until the end, not to begin to react while the other is still speaking. This means listening not only exteriorly but also interiorly until a person is finished, with a psychological maturity that is able to reason and speak without interrupting other persons in the conversation, avoiding using phrases such as "I would," "I'm against," "I don't agree," "I think rather," "I agree with," etc.

In discernment it is necessary to avoid this type of discussion between people precisely because it easily incites passionate thinking and leads to defending one's own point of view and to exaggerating the importance of one's vision or to discrediting another's opinion. In this way, community members are not more open, but begin to go back to being closed in on themselves and their own viewpoints or, at the most, those shared by only small groups. Discussion is certainly the most effective way of obstructing spiritual openness. For this reason it is useful to help ourselves with small rules in order not to fall into this snare. All members must be oriented to the Lord and with him toward the object of the discernment, avoiding relational impediments between people. The more we are tripped up in relationships, the less we are oriented in the right direction.

5. Also, there needs to be a superior, a guide for the community capable of carrying the process of discernment to a conclusion. This person should have a spiritual authority that is not simply *ex officio*, and he or she should know the dynamics of discernment in order to be able to guide the process.

The Immediate Preparation for Communal Discernment

- First of all, there must be an object for the discernment, something that is evidently good, in the spirit of the Gospel and the teaching of the Church, but that above all concerns the community in such an existential and profound way that many realities depend upon this decision. It must therefore be a question that regards God's will for the community.
- The superior should listen to all the members of the community individually in order to invite all of

them to begin to enter into a process of reflection and freedom, of testing if Christ and their love for him, etc., are the priorities in this issue.

At the end of these individual conversations, the superior should explain the object for discernment in a very concise, brief manner. He or she should present the object for discernment without using emotional words—words that could in some way influence others to take sides—but in a placid, terse style. It should be done in writing so that each member of the community can have it to read, pray, and reflect over.

- It is better to encourage solitude during the preparatory process, without having gatherings about the topic. If the members of the community speak about it among themselves, which is good, they should only speak one-on-one, never repeating what others have told them and commenting about their agreement, etc. Each person should only express his or her own opinion and listen to that of the other person without communicating this opinion to a third party or offering evaluations that have to do with particular people, for example: "It seems to me that the superior has not understood well," or "It's clear that many in the community don't understand what's at stake," etc.

- Every day the community members should spend an hour in prayer, possibly following the structure outlined in Part I of this volume, concluding with a written exam in order to have some evidence of how their souls move them and how they perceive these spiritual movements. As regards the content of prayer, it is an invocation to the Holy Spirit for illumination and for light, as well as for freedom and love for Christ. Therefore, it should be a prayer of contemplation of Christ's paschal mystery, to steep themselves in his way of acting, thinking, feeling, and willing.

It is fundamental always to safeguard an ecclesial dimension even in our prayer, considering the needs of the Church and the indications of the magisterium regarding the matter to be discerned. This is important because of the underlying aspect of Christianity, which is the incarnation and trans-figuration of reality and history in Christ.

- The members may also consult, with much discretion, a wise and prudent person in the form of spiritual dialogue.

How Communal Discernment Unfolds

- The superior presiding over the discernment gathers the community in the chapel for a time of prayer that he or she guides. It is a prayer to the Holy Spirit based on a passage from Sacred Scripture that in some way has to do with the matter being discerned. Internally, the prayer sets forth these passages in relation to freedom of will, to the paschal mentality, etc. This meditation, which unfolds in silence after the superior's introduction, may even last a half hour.

- Afterward the community gathers for conversation. Whoever is leading opens the process, presenting the matter for discernment concisely, without comments or emphasis.

- A person is chosen as secretary to write down everything that is said.

- Everyone's opinion is heard, preferably one after the other in a circle. Each person is invited to speak briefly and calmly, laying out only his or her personal opinion. No one should use words of confrontation or dialectic, but express only what relates to the matter at hand.

- After the first round, the guide, who thoroughly follows the process by observing where the consensus is moving, invites all present to participate in a second round in which members take from the first round any opinion other than their own that seems most right to them.

  When a members speaks, he or she should not name the person who expressed the opinion the member is now taking up, but should simply welcome the proposal and explain it in his or her own words and, in considering that opinion, perhaps add the things that come to mind and seem important to him or her. In this way an opinion begins to gain the consensus of many. Even if at the beginning that opinion was expressed through the affirmation of two people, it slowly acquires the consensus of many and is deepened, broadened, and encompasses realities that make it a truly solid opinion, always more complete and an expression of the community.

- There can be several more rounds, until a consensus is practically total.

- The guide, the whole time observing where the spiritual consensus is being formed, concludes by clearly defining the result and asking if the community is in agreement with how the content of the decision has been reached.

  In this way, the community can be sure that the decision is not an affirmation of some member of the community because he or she knows how to speak well, is influential, or knows how to threaten or persuade the others, but that the most spiritual proposal has been brought forth because consensus has been reached, which is the typical work of the Holy Spirit.

- In the case where coming to consensus is not so easy and the differences between some persons are strong, the guide can interrupt the process and again lead the community in prayer for liberation from personal opinions and viewpoints. Then the process restarts with a new round.

- If the process is still blocked, it is helpful, after yet another time of prayer, for the members of the group to listen to each other saying first only the spiritual advantages, then the disadvantages of deciding in favor of the matter in question. Then the community can return to prayer and begin once again to speak of the advantages and then disadvantages of deciding against the matter in question.

- Afterward the guide proposes a choice, deduced from the advantages, while also indicating the disadvantages. If all the members truly have an attitude of discernment, they should find consensus on that choice. When we talk about advantages and disadvantages in discernment, we are speaking exclusively about the community's greater surrender to Christ, the greater conformity to Christ of all the community's members, and a greater presence of Christ's salvation in the world through them.

Every advantage or disadvantage can be tested by uniting it to the Christ of the paschal triduum, since this is the way of the Master and his Bride, the Church. Consensus is a true collegial consensus. Even those members who saw more disadvantages than advantages in this decision will, in the end, adhere to it, making it their own, which is a true spiritual exercise. On paths such as these a community can come to the certainty that "it has seemed good to the Holy Spirit and to us" (cf. Acts 15:28).

Conclusion

THROUGH THIS VOLUME ON DISCERNMENT we have seen that everything has its fulcrum and verification in the passion of Jesus Christ. We have seen that discernment is an art of understanding oneself with God, of knowing oneself with the Lord. It is thus clear that discernment is not a technique with which we master God's language or his will. It has nothing to do with a methodology in the sense of modern sciences. Discernment, precisely because it is an art of communication between persons, cannot be reduced to a mere psychological approach for running our spiritual lives.

Sin has blocked communication between humanity and God. God, because he is love, gave himself into humanity's hands so that humanity could rediscover him, even if through an act of violence against the Son of God. The divine-human relationship is established anew in the sacrifice of Jesus, true God and true man, in his martyrdom, in his death at the hands of humanity. Jesus, obedient to the Father and given over into human hands, annihilates the chasm between the Father and humanity.

The Holy Spirit reveals to each person this event of reconciliation between humans and God. Baptism and Reconciliation, through which the Church brings her children to new life, are the perfect compass of God's merciful love. It is Christ's passion that reopens the communication between God and humanity and between humanity and God. It is the Holy Spirit who introduces us to the Passover of the Lamb. He is the Creator of our love toward God and toward others, and is, consequently, the Creator of divine-human understanding.

For this reason the first stage of discernment has its fulfillment in the acceptance of salvation. Following the thoughts and feelings suggested by the rules of discernment in the first stage, we come to admit the truth of our being sinners destined to death and isolated from life. This admission is possible when we have come to perceive the merciful Face of God who, in the passion of his Son, throws his arms around the penitent sinner. We memorize the taste, the flavor, the light, and the truth of Jesus Christ, Lord and Savior, imprinting him in our hearts in all his dimensions. This memory becomes the foundation for the following discernment.

We have also seen that Christian life remains bound to the passion and that the focus of discernment is an exercise of prayer through which we make the memory of Christ's passion penetrate us. That memory is the salvation we have experienced in an existential way, in our very ways of thinking, feeling, willing, and acting. It has to do with clothing ourselves anew in Christ, of having his feelings, of reasoning with him, and of desiring what he desires.

The temptations and deceptions of the enemy become more subtle. Our old selves reappear, and the enemy, with all his cunning, wants us to return to the culture of sin. Since he cannot trick us in a crude or mundane way, he tries to make us, while following Christ closely, disciples of Christ but in the manner of our old selves.

Following the path of this second stage of discernment, we reach that mentality of Christ's passion that enables us to recognize what is from Christ and what pretends to be such. Then the choices we make, be they important or trifling, are choices that make us Christlike. This means acquiring the wisdom to read history and events, and understanding how God carries out his plan of salvation through history.

> True discernment brings us to live an existence that will never again be released from the paschal mystery, in order that we might reach Christ's eternal passion.

Since this undertaking embraces the whole arc of the spiritual life, St. Ignatius bases the third and fourth week of the exercises entirely on the paschal mystery. It is not enough to dedicate only some period of our lives to the contemplation of Christ's passion; true discernment brings us to live an existence that will never again be released from the paschal mystery in order that we might reach Christ's eternal passion.

Therefore, discernment is an art with which we maintain the paschal attitude that is the place of encounter between humanity and God, which is the revelation of God, but also of humanity. God is love, and love is fulfilled in a paschal way. Men and women are the image of God and fulfill themselves in the way of the Son, in whom we are created and saved. Only the Holy Spirit makes us children of God. The Holy Spirit inspires us with thoughts of the Son so that we might acquire a filial way of reasoning. The Holy Spirit alone gives us the Son's feelings, and only with the love given to us by the Holy Spirit can these thoughts and feelings allow us to enter into the passion and to pass through to the end, to the resurrection. There is no spiritual access to the mystery of the passion, neither Christ's nor ours in Christ, without the Holy Spirit.

> *It is very clear that no virtue can come to full term*
> *or can endure without the grace of discernment...*
> *for discernment is the mother, the guardian,*
> *and the guide of all the virtues.*
> — John Cassian[1]

Notes

Introduction

1. Ancient Christian Writers: St. Maximus the Confessor, *The Four Centuries of Charity*, trans. Polycarp Sherwood, O.S.B. (London: Longmans, Green, and Co., 1955), 191.

2. For a historical look at discernment and a detailed treatment of it within the dimensions mentioned, see Manuel Ruíz Jurado, *El discernimiento espiritual: Teología, historia, práctica* (Madrid: Biblioteca de Autores Cristianos, 1994), and the article "Discernement des ésprits," in *Dictionnaire de spiritualité*, vol. 3 (Paris: Beauchesne, 1957), 1222–91. For a more practical-didactic aspect, see Silvano Fausti, *Occasione o tentazione? Arte di discernere e decidere* (Milan: Àncora, 1998).

3. I will indicate a few texts from spiritual authors that may constitute an excellent background to the theme: John Cassian, *On the Holy Fathers of Sketis and on Discrimination*, written for *Abba Leontios*, in *Philokalia*, 1:94–108; the writings of Nil Sorsky in *Nil Sorsky: The Complete Writings*, trans. George Maloney (Mahwah, NJ: Paulist Press, 2002); Ignatius of Loyola, *Autobiography*; Irenée Hausherr, *Philautie: De la tendresse pour soi à la chariteé selon saint Maxime le Confesseur* [Philautia: From Self-Love to Charity according to St. Maximus the Confessor] (Rome: Pont. Institutum Orientalium Studiorum, 1972); and Tomás Spidlík, *Ignazio di Loyola e la spiritualità orientale* [Ignatius of Loyola and Eastern Spirituality] (Rome: Studium, 1994).

PART I: ACQUIRING GOD'S TASTES

Chapter 1: The Basis of Discernment

1. Tomás Spidlík, *The Spirituality of the Christian East: A Systematic Handbook* (Kalamazoo, MI: Cistercian Publications, 1986), 29–34; Pavel Florenskij, *La colonna e il fondamento della verità* (Milan: Rusconi, 1974), 153–88; Michelina Tenace, *Dire l'uomo*, vol. 2, *Dall'immagine di Dio alla somiglianza* [Speaking the Human, vol. 2, From God's Image to Likeness] (Rome: Lipa Edizioni, 1997), 17–44.

2. Pavel Evdokimov, "L'Esprit-Saint et l'Église d'après la tradition liturgique" [The Holy Spirit and the Church in the Liturgical Tradition], in *L'Esprit-Saint et l'Église* (Paris: Fayard, 1969), 98.

3. See, for example, Sebastian Brock, *The Luminous Eye: The Spiritual World Vision of Saint Ephrem the Syrian* (Kalamazoo, MI: Cistercian Publications, 1992), 40–43.

4. Cf. Vjaceslav Ivanov, *Ty esi* [You Are], in Vladimir Solov'ëv, *Sobranie Socinenii*, vol. 3 (Brussels: Foyer Oriental Chrétien, 1979), 263–68, and Ivanov, *Anima* [Soul] in *Sobranie Socinenii*, 3:270–93.

5. See the entire function of matter in salvation as it emerges in Eastern theology as instrument and context for God's salvific power and the summation of all creation in Christ. For example, see the continuing emphasis on this aspect in diverse authors throughout the ages: John of Damascus, *On Holy Images*, 1.16; Nicholas Cabasilas, *Life in Christ*, trans. Margaret Lisney (London: Janus, 1989), 38; Solov'ëv, *Sobranie Socinenii*, vol. 6 (1966), 35ff. See Tomás Spidlík, "Solov'ëv," in *La mistica, fenomenologia e riflessione teologica*, ed. Ermanno Ancilli, Maurizio Paparozzi (Rome: Città Nuova Editrice, 1984), 658ff.; Alexander Schmemann, *The World as Sacrament* (London: Darton, Longman, and Todd, 1966); John Zizioulas, *Being as Communion* (Crestwood, NY: St. Vladimir's Press, 1985).

6. See Athanasius, *Ad Serap.*, ep. 3.

7. See Tomás Spidlík, *Noi nella Trinità: Breve saggio sulla Trinità* [We in the Trinity: Brief Essay on the Trinity] (Rome: Lipa Edizioni, 2000).

8. On this point see Marko I. Rupnik, *Dire l'uomo*, vol. 1, *Per una cultura della pasqua*, 2nd ed. [Speaking the Human, vol. 1, Toward a Paschal Culture] (Rome: Lipa Edizioni, 1997), 77–89.

9. See Sergius Bulgakov, "Glavy o troicnosti" [Chapters on Trinitarity], *Pravoslavnaja Mysl'* 1 (1928): 66–70; Sergius Bulgakov, *Agnets bozhii* [The Lamb of God], part 1 of *O bogochelovechestve* (Paris: YMCA Press, 1933), translated into Italian as *L'Agnello di Dio* (Rome: Città Nuova, 1990), 161–62; Bulgakov, *Utesitel'* (Paris: YMCA Press, 1936), translated into Italian as *Il Paraclito* [The Paraclete] (Bologna: Dehoniane, 1971), 345–50. See also Giuseppe Maria Zanghí, *Dio che è amore: Trinità e vita in Cristo* [God Who Is Love: Trinity and Life in Christ] (Rome: Città Nuova, 1991), 78; and Anastasio Jevtis, *L'infinito cammino: Umanazione di Dio e deificazione dell'uomo* [The Infinite Path: The Humanization of God and the Deification of the Human] (Sotto il Monte-Schio: Servitium Editrice, 1996), 195–252.

10. Vladimir Solov'ëv, *Kritika otvlecënniych nacal* [The Critique of Abstract Principles], in *Sobranie Socinenii*, vol. 2 (1966), translated into Italian as *La critica dei principi astratti* (1877–1880), in *Sulla Divinoumanità e altri scritti* (Milan: Jaca, 1971), 197–210.

11. See Vladimir Solov'ëv, *Il significato dell'amore e altri scritti* (Milan: La Casa di Matrona, 1983), 88–101, originally published as *Smysl ljubvi*, in *Sobranie Socinenii*, vol. 7 (1966), trans. Thomas R. Beyer, Jr. as *The Meaning of Love* (Hudson, NY: Lindisfarne Press, 1985).

12. Vladimir Solov'ëv, *Duchovnja osnovy zizni*, in *Sobranie Socinenii*, vol. 3 (1966), trans. Donald Attwater as *God, Man and the Church: The Spiritual Foundations of Life* (Milwaukee: Bruce Publishing Co., 1938), 21–34.

13. See Vladimir Ivanov, *Dostoevskij: Tragedija—Mif—Mistika* [Dostoyevsky: Tragedy, Myth, Mysticism], in *Sobranie Socinenii*, vol. 4 (1987), 503–55.

14. Sec Ephrem the Syrian, *Hymns on Faith*, 31, partial trans. Brock, *Luminous Eye*, 60–62.

15. See Bulgakov, *Il Paraclito*, 143–46.

16. See Olivier Clément, *The Roots of Christian Mysticism: Texts from the Patristic Era with Commentary*, trans. Theodore Berkeley (New York: New City Press, 1995), 76-91.

17. On this see the abundant patristic references in Myrrha Lot-Borodine, *La déification de l'homme selon la doctrine des Pères grecs* [The Deification of the Human in the Teaching of the Greek Fathers] (Paris: Cerf, 1970).

18. See Rupnik, *Cultura della pasqua*, 71–109.

19. See Sergius Bulgakov, *La luce senza tramonto* [The Unfading Light] (Rome: Lipa Edizioni, 2002), 380–88.

20. Nikolai Berdiaev, *De l'esclavage et de la liberté de l'homme* (Paris: Aubier, 1946), 20-25, (translated by Reginald M. French as *Slavery and Freedom* (New York: C. Scribner's Sons, 1944).

21. See Basil, *In Hexameron*, 9.2.

22. See Rupnik, *Cultura della pasqua*, 169–73.

23. Sec Sergius Bulgakov, *The Orthodox Church*, trans. Lydia Kesich (Crestwood, NY: St. Vladimir's Seminary Press, 1988), 9–35.

Chapter 2: What Is Discernment?

1. On the relationship between the intellect and love, see Rupnik, *Cultura della pasqua*, 143ff.

2. See the entry "noûs" in *Dictionnaire de spiritualité*, vol. 11 (1982), 459–69.

3. See Tomás Spidlík, "Il cuore nella spiritualità dell'oriente cristiano" [The Heart in the Spirituality of the Christian East], in Tomás Spidlík, Maria Campitelli, et al., *Lezioni sulla Divinoumanità* [Lessons in Divine Love] (Rome: Lipa Edizioni, 1995), 83–98.

4. See Simeon L. Frank, "La realtà e l'uomo: Metafisica dell'essere umano," in *Il pensiero religioso russo: Da Tolstoj a Lossky*, ed. Pietro Modesto (Milan: Vita e Pensiero, 1997),

262–77, trans. Natalie Duddington as *Reality and Man: An Essay in the Metaphysics of Human Nature* (New York: Taplinger Publishing Co., 1965).

5. See Marko I. Rupnik, "Paralelismos entre el discernimiento según san Ignacio y el discernimiento según algunos autores de la Filocalia" [Parallelisms between Discernment according to St. Ignatius and Discernment According to Some Philokalic Authors], in *Las fuentes de los Ejercicios espirituales de san Ignacio*, ed. Juan Plazaola (Bilbao: Ediciones Mensajero, 1998), 241–80.

6. See Marko I. Rupnik, *In the Fire of the Burning Bush: An Initiation to the Spiritual Life*, trans. Susan Dawson Vásquez (Grand Rapids: Eerdmans, 2004), 105–9.

Chapter 3: The Dynamics of the First Stage of Discernment

1. The pages that follow are the development of a long reflection beginning from the texts of St. Ignatius—mainly the rules for the first week of the *Spiritual Exercises* (from *Ignatius of Loyola: The Spiritual Exercises and Selected Works*, trans. George E. Ganss (Mahwah, NJ: Paulist Press, 1991), 113–214; his autobiography (in *A Pilgrim's Journey: The Autobiography of Ignatius of Loyola*, trans. Joseph Tylenda (San Francisco: Ignatius Press, 2001); and some of the letters (in Ignatius of Loyola, *Letters*, trans. William J. Young (Chicago: Loyola University Press, 1959)—from texts of mainly philokalic authors—such as Diadochus of Photiki, *On Spiritual Knowledge and Discrimination: One Hundred Texts*, in *Philokalia*, vol. 1, ed. G. E. H. Palmer, Philip Sherrard, Kallistos Ware (London: Faber and Faber, 1979), 251–96; Symeon Metaphrastis, *Paraphrase of the Homilies of St. Makarios of Egypt*, in *Philokalia*, vol. 3 (1984), 282–354; *A Discourse on Abba Philimon*, in *Philokalia*, vol. 2 (1981), 344–57; John Cassian's *conferences*, in *John Cassian: Conferences*, trans. Colm Luibheid (Mahwah, NJ: Paulist Press, 1985); and Maximus the Confessor, *Centuries on Charity*, in St. Maximus the Confessor, *The Ascetic Life, The Four Centuries on Charity*, trans. Polycarp Sherwood, O.S.B.

(Mahwah, NJ: Paulist Press, 1955)—and from my twenty-five years of experience of guided spiritual exercises.

2. See Rupnik, *Cultura della pasqua*, 179–225.

3. See Marko I. Rupnik, *Gli si gettò al collo* [And Threw His Arms Around Him] (Rome: Lipa Edizioni, 1997), 43–45.

4. As a possible example, see Rupnik, *Gli si gettò al collo;* Marko I. Rupnik, *Cerco i miei fratelli* [I am Seeking My Brothers and Sisters] (Rome: Lipa Edizioni, 1997); or Genesis 3–4 and the Passion of Christ in Rupnik, *Cultura della pasqua*, 227–71.

PART II: HOW TO REMAIN WITH CHRIST

Chapter 4: The Principle and Foundation of Discerning How to Remain in Christ

1. See Solov'ëv, *God, Man and the Church*, 113–31; Vladimir Truhlar, "Odresenje," in *Leksikon duhovnosti* (Celje: Queriniana, 1974), 392; Rupnik, *Cultura della pasqua*, 227–71.

2. Obviously, the two stages of discernment, or rather the two principal phases of growth in the spiritual life—the purgative and the creative in following Christ—are not so absolutely separate. The spiritual authors speak of them in this style for a greater understanding of how the spirits work on us and how we behave when God draws near or when we are tempted. The person is an organism, not a concept. Therefore, our stages of growth cannot be characterized in a simple, mathematical way. Growth and maturity become manifest through varying connotations that indicate a person's particular movements and contents.

3. Mark the Ascetic, *Letter to Nicolas the Solitary*, in *Philokalia*, 1:148; Diadochus of Photiki, *On Spiritual Knowledge*, 30.

4. Ignatius of Loyola, *Spiritual Exercises*, 329, 335; cf. the rule of the ancient ascetics *quidquid inquietat est a diabolo*. See also Athanasius, *Life of Antony*, 36, in *Athanasius: The Life of Antony and Letter to Marcellinus*, trans. Robert C. Gregg,

(Mahwah, NJ: Paulist Press, 1980), 58, and Evagrius of Ponticus, *Prakticos*, 80, *The Prakticos and Chapters on Prayer*, trans. John Eudes Bamberger, (Kalamazoo, MI: Cistercian Publications, 1981), 36.

5. This appellative has its origin in ancient Christianity, where the Western binomial natural/supernatural had the meaning of human/divine or created/uncreated. This highlighted the fact that evil is not natural to humanity and is not an integral part of humanity as created by God. According to the ancient Fathers, in fact, human nature not only is good but participates in divine life, and thus humanity living according to its nature realizes the ideal of spiritual life. The expression "enemy of human nature" is used precisely to avoid a Manichean vision of spiritual life, in that humanity is not exposed to the influence of two equal powers that act upon it. See Spidlík, *Spirituality of the Christian East*, 62–64.

6. Symeon Metaphrastis, *Paraphrase*, 122; Diadochus of Photiki, *On Spiritual Knowledge*, 36, 40.

Chapter 5: Temptations

1. Evagrius formulated the famous list of eight capital sins (gluttony, lust, avarice, discontent, wrath, despondency, vainglory, and pride). In the West, after Cassian, this list was borrowed by Gregory the Great and had wide success with some changes until the thirteenth century, when the classification stabilized into the seven capital sins now known in the West. Cf. Spidlík, *Spirituality of the Christian East*, 248–49.

2. Origen, *Fragm. In Johannes*, 9, in *Die Griechischen Christlichen Schriftsteller*, Origines 4, 490; Symeon Metaphrastis, *Paraphrase*, 11, 135; Diadochus of Photiki, *On Spiritual Knowledge*, 20–21; *The Sayings of the Desert Fathers*, trans. Benedicta Ward (Kalamazoo, MI: Cistercian Publications, 1975), 3 (Anthony, 8); Solov'ëv, *God, Man, and the Church*, 21–34.

3. Diadochus of Photiki, *On Spiritual Knowledge*, 31, 36, 38; Ignatius of Loyola, *Autobiography*, 19–20; Ignatius of Loyola, *Spiritual Exercises*, 331, 333; Seraphim of Sarov,

Spiritual Instructions, vol. 1 of *Little Russian Philokalia* (Ouzinkie, AK: St. Herman Press, 1991), 86; Theophan the Recluse, "The Fruits of Prayer," in Caritone of Valamo, *The Art of Prayer: An Orthodox Anthology*, trans. E. Kadloubovsky and E. M. Palmer (London: Faber and Faber, 1966), 132.

4. Dorotheos of Gaza, *Life of St. Dositheus*; Dorotheos of Gaza, *Spiritual Teachings*, 5.66. The works of St. Dorotheos can be found in *Oeuvres spirituelles*, ed. Lucien Regnault (Paris: Cerf, 2001), *Sources Chrètiennes*, 92.

5. Dorotheos of Gaza, *Spiritual Teachings*, 5.61–68, 5.105–14, 6.71, 6.74–75, 6.77, 6.117, 6.120–21, 6.123–24; *Sayings of the Desert Fathers*, 102 (Joseph of Panephysis, 2), 75 (Poemen, 64); Maximus the Confessor, *Centuries on Charity*, 2.49, 3.39, 3.54–55, 3.84; Ignatius of Loyola, *Autobiography*, 15.

6. Symeon Metaphrastis, *Paraphrase*, 147; Maximus the Confessor, *Ad Thalassium, Praef.*; Ignatius of Loyola, *Spiritual Exercises*, 332; Hausherr, *Philautía*, 81–150; Spidlík, *Spirituality of the Christian East*, 94–96.

7. Symeon Metaphrastis, *Paraphrase*, 110, 115; Maximus the Confessor, *Centuries on Charity*, 2.46, 3.48, 3.75; Ignatius of Loyola, *Constitutions*, General Examen, 101, in *Spiritual Exercises and Selected Works*; Ignatius of Loyola, *Spiritual Exercises*, 322; Archimandrite Sophrony (Sakharov), *St. Silouan the Athonite*, trans. Rosemary Edwards (Crestwood, NY: St. Vladimir's Seminary Press, 1999), 116.

Chapter 6: How to Conquer Temptations

1. Tomás Spidlík, *Manuale fondamentale di spiritualità* [Basic Manual of Spirituality] (Casale Monferrato: Piemme, 1993), 421–24.

2. Dorotheos of Gaza, *Spiritual Teachings*, 5.66, 5.110–11; Ignatius of Loyola, *Spiritual Excercises*, 17, 22, 326; Irenée Hausherr, *Direction spirituelle en Orient autrefois* [Spiritual Direction in the East in Former Times] (Rome: Edizioni Orientalia, 1955), 212ff.; Tomás Spidlík, "La direzione spirituale nell'Oriente cristiano" [Spiritual Direction in Eastern

Christianity], in *In Colloquio* [In Dialogue] (Rome: Lipa Edizioni, 1995), 11–54; Rupnik, *Fire of the Burning Bush*, 91–111.

3. Mark the Ascetic, *Letter to Nicolas the Solitary;* Diadochus of Photiki, *On Spiritual Knowledge*, 30; Ignatius of Loyola, *Spiritual Exercises*, 230–37; and H. J. Sieben, "Mnèmè Theou," in *Dictionnaire de Spiritualité*, vol. 10 (1980), 1407–14.

4. Ignatius of Loyola, *Spiritual Exercises*, 352; Dumitru Staniloaë, *Il genio dell'ortodossia* (Milan: Jaca Book, 1986), 79–125; Robert F. Taft, *Beyond East and West* (Washington, D.C.: Pastoral Press, 1984), 111–26; and Robert F. Taft, *The Liturgy of the Hours in East and West* (Collegeville, MN: Liturgical Press, 1986), 367–73.

5. Diadochus of Photiki, *On Spiritual Knowledge*, 86, 90; *Sayings of the Desert Fathers*, 2 (Anthony, 5); Maximus the Confessor, *Centuries on Charity*, 2.67; Archimandrite Sophrony (Sakharov), *St. Silouan the Athonite.*

6. Ignatius of Loyola, *Spiritual Exercises*, 330; Tomás Spidlík, *Il cuore e lo spirito: La dottrina spirituale di Teofane il Recluso* [The Heart and the Spirit: The Spiritual Doctrine of Theophan the Recluse] (Vatican City: Libreria Editrice Vaticana, 2004), 302ff.; Spidlík, *Spirituality of the Christian East*, 312; Spidlík, *Ignazio di Loyola*, 86–88.

Chapter 7: Testing Our Free Surrender to Christ

1. See Rupnik, Ignatius of Loyola, 67–131. Editor's note: At times it is more faithful to the theological understanding of the Fathers of the Church and St. Paul to use the phrase "sons in the Son," despite its gender-specific language. St. Paul tells us that all of us, both male and female, become in Baptism members of the only-begotten Son and thus children of his heavenly Father, sons in the Son. Fashioned in his likeness (Rom 8:29) we cry "Abba, Father!" (Gal 4:6). "Son" refers always to both men and women.

2. Maximus the Confessor, *Centuries on Charity*, 1.94, 3.44, 4.40–41; Ignatius of Loyola, *Spiritual Exercises*, 136–47.

3. Ignatius of Loyola, *Spiritual Exercises*, 149–57; Solov'ëv, *God, Man, and the Church*, 35ff.

4. Symeon Metaphrastis, *Paraphrase*, 133, 136; Ignatius of Loyola, *Spiritual Exercises*, 164–68.

5. *A Discourse on Abba Philimon*, 345; Ignatius of Loyola, *Spiritual Exercises*, 135.

6. Hugo Rahner, *The Spirituality of St. Ignatius Loyola: An Account of its Historical Development*, trans. Francis John Smith (Westminster: Newman Press, 1953), 47; Rupnik, *Paralelismos entre el discernimiento*, 262–80.

7. Ignatius of Loyola, *Spiritual Exercises*, 170–74.

Chapter 8: Practicing Discernment

1. Ignatius of Loyola, *Spiritual Exercises*, 175–88.

Chapter 9: Vocation

1. John Climacus, *The Ladder of Divine Ascent*, 1.6, trans. Colm Luibheid and Norman Russell (Mahwah, NJ: Paulist Press, 1982), 74–75; Rupnik, *Fire of the Burning Bush*, 66–67.

Chapter 10: Communal Discernment

1. Symeon Metaphrastis, *Paraphrase*, 27.

Conclusion

1. John Cassian, *Conferences*, 2.4, in *John Cassian: Conferences*, 64.

BOOKS & MEDIA

The Daughters of St. Paul operate book and media centers at the following addresses. Visit, call, or write the one nearest you today, or find us at www.pauline.org.

CALIFORNIA
3908 Sepulveda Blvd, Culver City, CA 90230 — 310-397-8676
935 Brewster Avenue, Redwood City, CA 94063 — 650-369-4230

FLORIDA
145 S.W. 107th Avenue, Miami, FL 33174 — 305-559-6715

HAWAII
1143 Bishop Street, Honolulu, HI 96813 — 808-521-2731

ILLINOIS
172 North Michigan Avenue, Chicago, IL 60601 — 312-346-4228

LOUISIANA
4403 Veterans Memorial Blvd, Metairie, LA 70006 — 504-887-7631

MASSACHUSETTS
885 Providence Hwy, Dedham, MA 02026 — 781-326-5385

MISSOURI
9804 Watson Road, St. Louis, MO 63126 — 314-965-3512

NEW YORK
64 W. 38th Street, New York, NY 10018 — 212-754-1110

SOUTH CAROLINA
243 King Street, Charleston, SC 29401 — 843-577-0175

TEXAS
Currently no book center; for parish exhibits or outreach evangelization, contact: 210-569-0500, or SanAntonio@paulinemedia.com, or P.O. Box 761416, San Antonio, TX 78245

VIRGINIA
1025 King Street, Alexandria, VA 22314 — 703-549-3806

CANADA
3022 Dufferin Street, Toronto, ON M6B 3T5 — 416-781-9131

¡También somos su fuente para libros,
videos y música en español!